# BRITISH HISTORY ATLAS

# BRITISH HISTORY ATLAS

## Martin Gilbert
*Fellow of Merton College, Oxford*

Cartography by ARTHUR BANKS

Weidenfeld and Nicolson
5 Winsley Street London W1

**Printed** by Ebenezer Baylis & Son, Ltd.,
Worcester, and London

# Preface

The maps in this atlas are intended to provide a visual introduction to British history. I have used the word 'British' in its widest scope, including when relevant England, Scotland, Ireland and Wales, the changing overseas empire, the wars and treaties in which Britain engaged, the alliances in time of peace, the growth of industry and trade, and, on five of the maps, famine and plague.

The story of the British Isles forms the central theme. I have included maps to illustrate economic, social and political problems as well as territorial and military ones. I hope this atlas will help to show that there is more to British history than Hastings and Crécy, Blenheim and Waterloo, Passchendaele and Dunkirk, all of which moments of glory I have tried to put in their wider, and no less important, contexts.

For the maps covering the period before the Norman Conquest the sources are often conflicting on specific details. I have therefore drawn these maps on the basis of probability. In many instances precise knowledge of early frontiers is lacking. I have tried nevertheless to give a clear if also, of necessity, an approximate picture.

As British history advances from wattle huts to timber mansions, and thence on to steel and concrete, so too do the number and variety of facts available to the historian. This is reflected in the maps themselves. I have tried to avoid too complex or too cluttered a page; but a map cannot always satisfy all the demands made upon it, and only the reader can judge where clarity of design and sufficiency of information have been successfully combined.

I am under an obligation of gratitude to those historians and colleagues who kindly scrutinised my draft maps at an early stage, and who made many suggestions for their scope and improvement; in particular Dr J. M. Wallace-Hadrill, Dr Roger Highfield, Mr Ralph Davis, Mr T. F. R. G. Braun, Dr C. C. Davies and Miss Barbara Malament. When the maps were more completed, they were checked by Mr Adrian Scheps, Mr Edmund Ranallo, Mrs Elizabeth Goold, Mr Tony Lawdham and Mrs Jean Kelly, to all of whom my thanks are due.

Both the publishers and I are beholden to the cartographic skill and energy of Mr Arthur Banks, who transformed rough drafts, pencil sketches and complex instructions into maps of the highest clarity and most attractive design.

I should greatly welcome any corrections of these maps for future editions.

MARTIN GILBERT
*Merton College, Oxford*

1968

# List of Maps

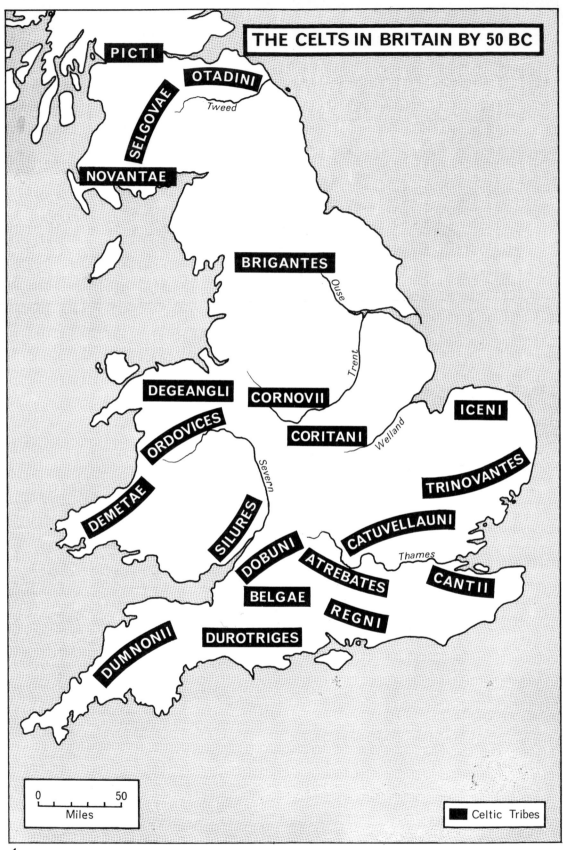

THE CELTS IN BRITAIN BY 50 BC

PICTI

OTADINI

SELGOVAE

*Tweed*

NOVANTAE

BRIGANTES

*Ouse*

*Trent*

DEGEANGLI

CORNOVII

ICENI

CORITANI

*Welland*

ORDOVICES

TRINOVANTES

*Severn*

DEMETAE

SILURES

CATUVELLAUNI

*Thames*

DOBUNI

ATREBATES

CANTII

BELGAE

REGNI

DUMNONII

DUROTRIGES

0    50
Miles

■ Celtic Tribes

1

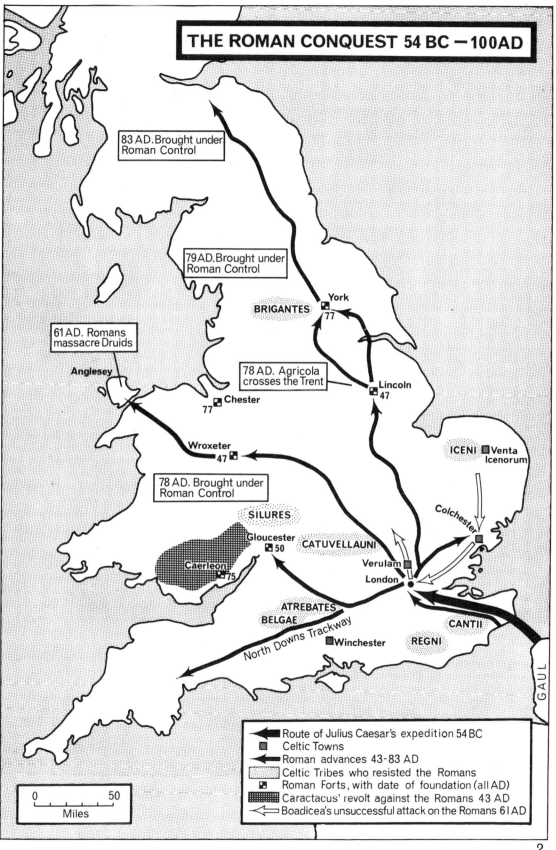

# THE ROMAN CONQUEST 54 BC — 100AD

83 AD. Brought under Roman Control

79 AD. Brought under Roman Control

BRIGANTES

York
77

61 AD. Romans massacre Druids

Anglesey

78 AD. Agricola crosses the Trent

Chester
77

Lincoln
47

Wroxeter
47

78 AD. Brought under Roman Control

ICENI   Venta Icenorum

SILURES

Gloucester
50

CATUVELLAUNI

Colchester

Caerleon
75

Verulam

London

ATREBATES
BELGAE

North Downs Trackway

CANTII

Winchester

REGNI

GAUL

Miles

0   50

◄— Route of Julius Caesar's expedition 54 BC
▦ Celtic Towns
◀— Roman advances 43-83 AD
Celtic Tribes who resisted the Romans
▣ Roman Forts, with date of foundation (all AD)
▓ Caractacus' revolt against the Romans 43 AD
⇐ Boadicea's unsuccessful attack on the Romans 61 AD

2

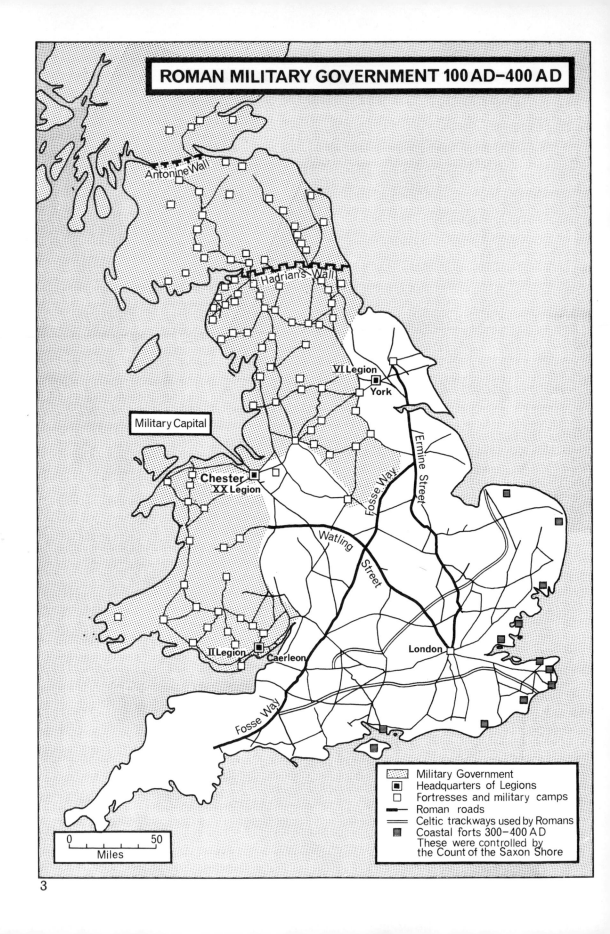

# ROMAN MILITARY GOVERNMENT 100 AD–400 AD

Antonine Wall

Hadrian's Wall

**VI Legion**
York

Military Capital

**Chester**
**XX Legion**

Fosse Way

Ermine Street

Watling Street

**II Legion**
Caerleon

London

Fosse Way

| | Military Government |
| ■ | Headquarters of Legions |
| □ | Fortresses and military camps |
| — | Roman roads |
| ═ | Celtic trackways used by Romans |
| ▧ | Coastal forts 300–400 A D |

These were controlled by
the Count of the Saxon Shore

0        50
Miles

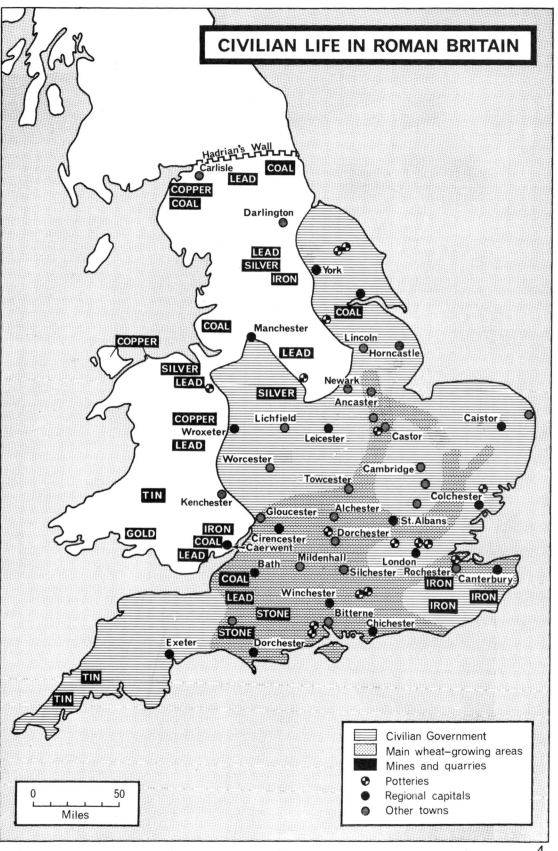

# CIVILIAN LIFE IN ROMAN BRITAIN

Hadrian's Wall

Carlisle  **LEAD**  **COAL**

**COPPER**
**COAL**

Darlington

**LEAD**
**SILVER**
**IRON**

York

**COAL**

**COAL**

Manchester

Lincoln

**LEAD**

Horncastle

**COPPER**

Newark

**SILVER**
**LEAD**

**SILVER**

Ancaster

**COPPER**

Lichfield

Caistor

Wroxeter

Leicester

Castor

**LEAD**

Worcester

Cambridge

Towcester

Colchester

**TIN**

Kenchester

Alchester

Gloucester

St. Albans

**GOLD**

Dorchester

**IRON**
**COAL**

Cirencester

**LEAD**

Caerwent

Mildenhall

London

Bath

Silchester   Rochester

**COAL**

Winchester

**IRON**   Canterbury

**LEAD**

**IRON**   **IRON**

**STONE**

Bitterne

**STONE**

Chichester

Exeter

Dorchester

**TIN**

**TIN**

| | Civilian Government |
| --- | --- |
| | Main wheat–growing areas |
| | Mines and quarries |
| | Potteries |
| | Regional capitals |
| | Other towns |

0    50
Miles

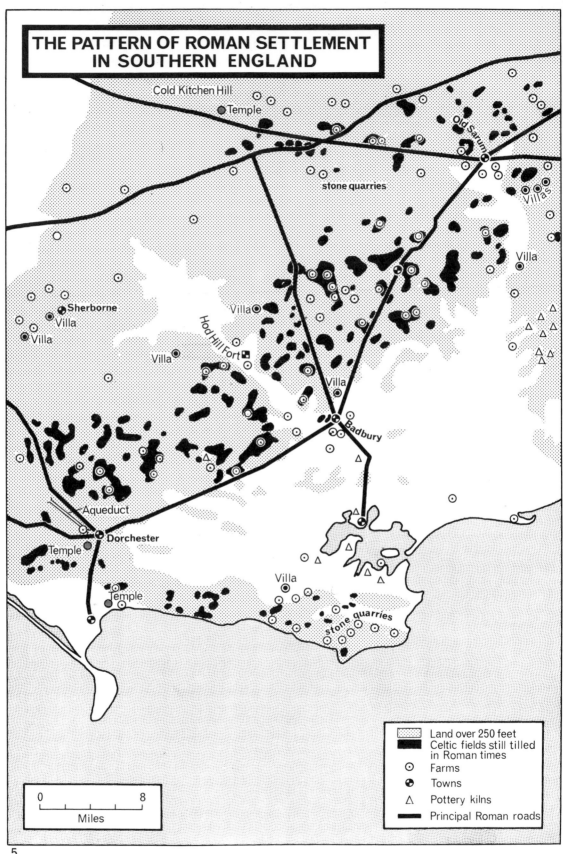

# THE PATTERN OF ROMAN SETTLEMENT IN SOUTHERN ENGLAND

Cold Kitchen Hill

Temple

Old Sarum

stone quarries

Villas

Villa

Sherborne

Villa

Villa

Villa

Hod Hill Fort

Villa

Villa

Villa

Badbury

Aqueduct

Dorchester

Temple

Temple

Villa

stone quarries

Land over 250 feet

Celtic fields still tilled in Roman times

⊙ Farms

◉ Towns

△ Pottery kilns

▬ Principal Roman roads

0 ____ 8
Miles

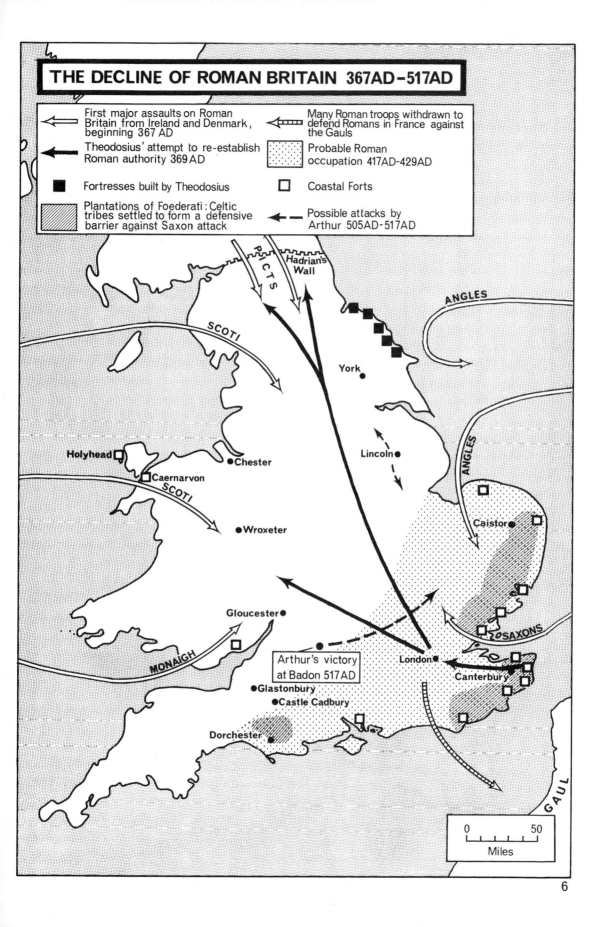

# THE DECLINE OF ROMAN BRITAIN 367AD–517AD

⟵ First major assaults on Roman Britain from Ireland and Denmark, beginning 367 AD

⟵ Theodosius' attempt to re-establish Roman authority 369 AD

■ Fortresses built by Theodosius

▨ Plantations of Foederati: Celtic tribes settled to form a defensive barrier against Saxon attack

⟵ Many Roman troops withdrawn to defend Romans in France against the Gauls

⬚ Probable Roman occupation 417AD–429AD

☐ Coastal Forts

⟵ Possible attacks by Arthur 505AD–517AD

PICTS

Hadrian's Wall

ANGLES

SCOTI

York

ANGLES

Holyhead ☐

Chester ●

Caernarvon ☐

SCOTI

Lincoln ●

Caistor ●

Wroxeter ●

Gloucester ●

SAXONS

MONAIGH

London ●

Arthur's victory at Badon 517AD

Canterbury ☐

Glastonbury ●
Castle Cadbury ☐

Dorchester ●

GAUL

0        50
Miles

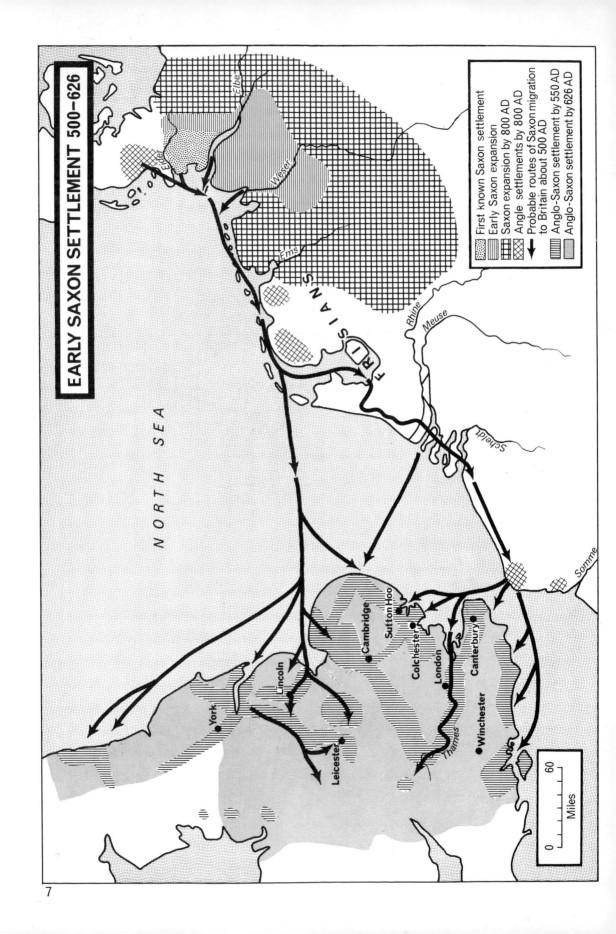

# EARLY SAXON SETTLEMENT 500–626

Elbe

Weser

Eider

Ems

Rhine

Meuse

Scheldt

Somme

F R I S I A N S

NORTH SEA

York

Lincoln

Leicester

Cambridge

Sutton Hoo

Colchester

London

Canterbury

Winchester

Thames

First known Saxon settlement
Early Saxon expansion
Saxon expansion by 800 AD
Angle settlements by 800 AD
Probable routes of Saxon migration to Britain about 500 AD
Anglo-Saxon settlement by 550 AD
Anglo-Saxon settlement by 626 AD

0        60

Miles

# SAXON KINGDOMS AND BRETWALDASHIPS 630-829

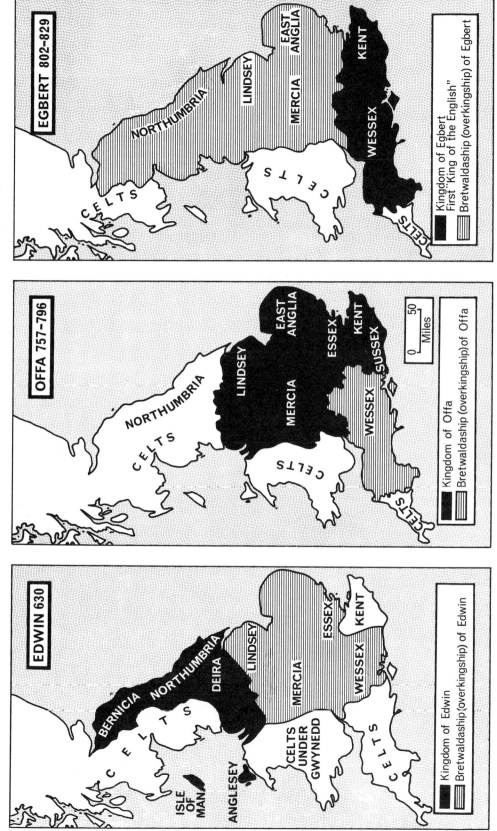

**EGBERT 802-829**

NORTHUMBRIA
LINDSEY
MERCIA
EAST ANGLIA
KENT
WESSEX
CELTS
CELTS

■ Kingdom of Egbert
First 'King of the English'
▨ Bretwaldaship (overkingship) of Egbert

**OFFA 757-796**

NORTHUMBRIA
CELTS
LINDSEY
MERCIA
EAST ANGLIA
ESSEX
KENT
SUSSEX
WESSEX
CELTS
CELTS

0    50
Miles

■ Kingdom of Offa
▨ Bretwaldaship (overkingship) of Offa

**EDWIN 630**

BERNICIA
NORTHUMBRIA
DEIRA
CELTS
LINDSEY
MERCIA
ESSEX
KENT
WESSEX
CELTS UNDER GWYNEDD
CELTS
ISLE OF MAN
ANGLESEY

■ Kingdom of Edwin
▨ Bretwaldaship (overkingship) of Edwin

8

THE CHURCH 700-850

† Abercorn
Coldingham ⊕
Lindisfarne
L I N D I S F A R N E
† Melrose
Coquet Island
WHITHORN
† Tynemouth
† Jarrow
Hexham † Monkwearmouth
HEXHAM
⊕ Whithorn
⊕ Hartlepool
† Gainford
† Whitby
† Sockburn
Gilling
Lastingham † Hackness †
Y O R K
† Ripon
York
† Barrow
Syddensis Civitas
(site not known)
L I N D S E Y
LICHFIELD
Elmham
Repton ⊕ † Breedon
E L M H A M
Lichfield
Peterborough †
Leicester † Oundle Ely
† Brixworth
Dunwich
† Bury St.
Edmunds
L E I C E S T E R
DUNWICH
HEREFORD
Worcester
DORCHESTER
LONDON
WORCESTER
† Malmesbury
⊕ Barking
London
Recultur
Hereford
Dorchester
Abingdon
ROCH-
ESTER
Minster
† Dover
Canterbury
Folkestone
CANTER-
BURY
Lyminge
WINCHESTER
† Woking
Glastonbury †
Winchester
Sherborne
† Tisbury
SELSEY
SHERBORNE
Nursling †
Selsey
Exeter †
Wimborne †

† Religious houses founded by 850

⊕ Double houses where monks and nuns lived under the rule of an abbess

― Approximate diocesan boundaries

● Diocesan seats

▨ Archbishoprics

0        50
Miles

9

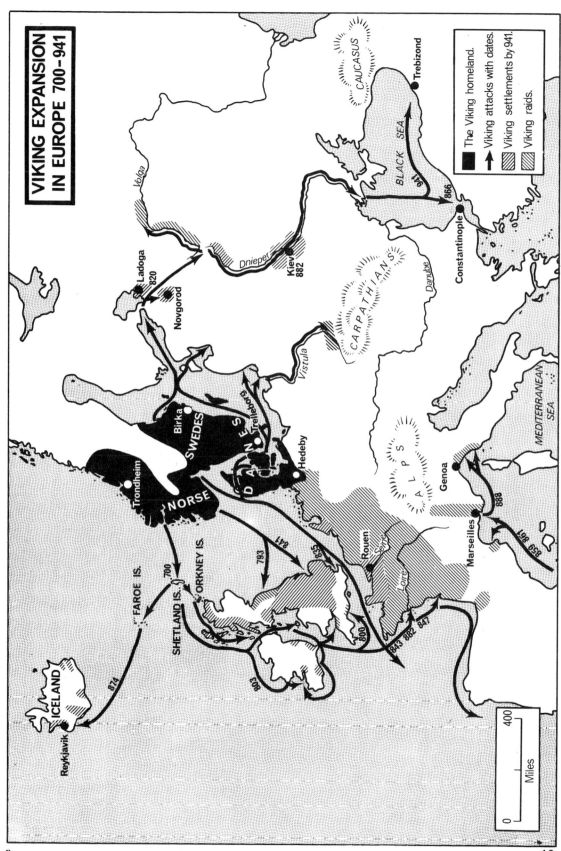

VIKING EXPANSION IN EUROPE 700–941

The Viking homeland.
Viking attacks with dates.
Viking settlements by 941.
Viking raids.

Trebizond

CAUCASUS

BLACK SEA

Volga

Dnieper

Kiev
882

Constantinople

666

CARPATHIANS

Ladoga
820

Novgorod

Danube

Vistula

MEDITERRANEAN SEA

Birka

SWEDES

Trelleborg

DANES

ALPS

Genoa

Hedeby

Trondheim

NORSE

Rouen

Seine

Marseilles

888

Loire

859 861

800

843 882 847

860

793

834

FAROE IS.

700

SHETLAND IS.

ORKNEY IS.

874

ICELAND

Reykjavik

893

Miles

0          400

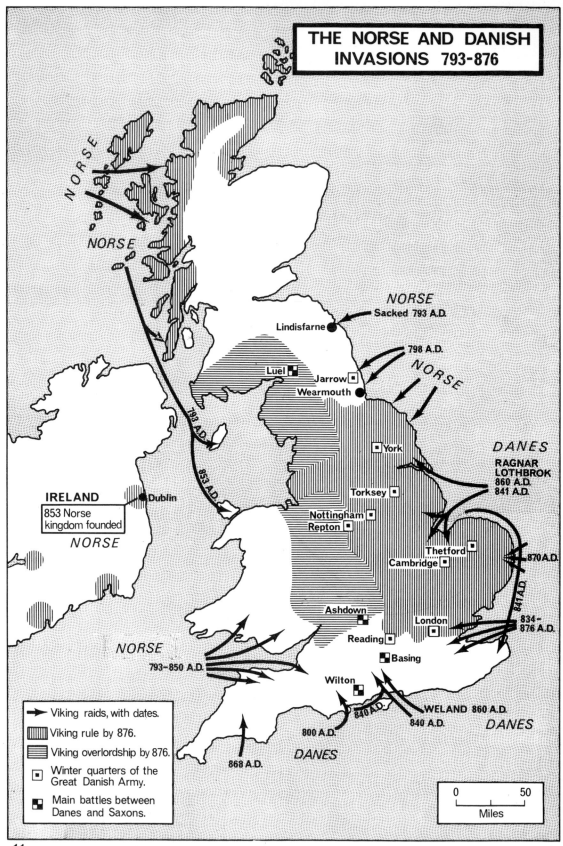

THE NORSE AND DANISH
INVASIONS 793-876

NORSE

NORSE

NORSE

NORSE
Lindisfarne  Sacked 793 A.D.

798 A.D.

NORSE

Luel  Jarrow
Wearmouth

DANES

York

RAGNAR
LOTHBROK
860 A.D.
841 A.D.

IRELAND  Dublin

853 Norse
kingdom founded

NORSE

Torksey

Nottingham
Repton

Thetford
Cambridge  870 A.D.

NORSE

Ashdown

London

834–
876 A.D.

Reading

Basing

Wilton

NORSE

WELAND 860 A.D.

793-850 A.D.

840 A.D.

840 A.D.

DANES

800 A.D.

868 A.D.

DANES

Viking raids, with dates.

Viking rule by 876.

Viking overlordship by 876.

Winter quarters of the
Great Danish Army.

Main battles between
Danes and Saxons.

0      50
Miles

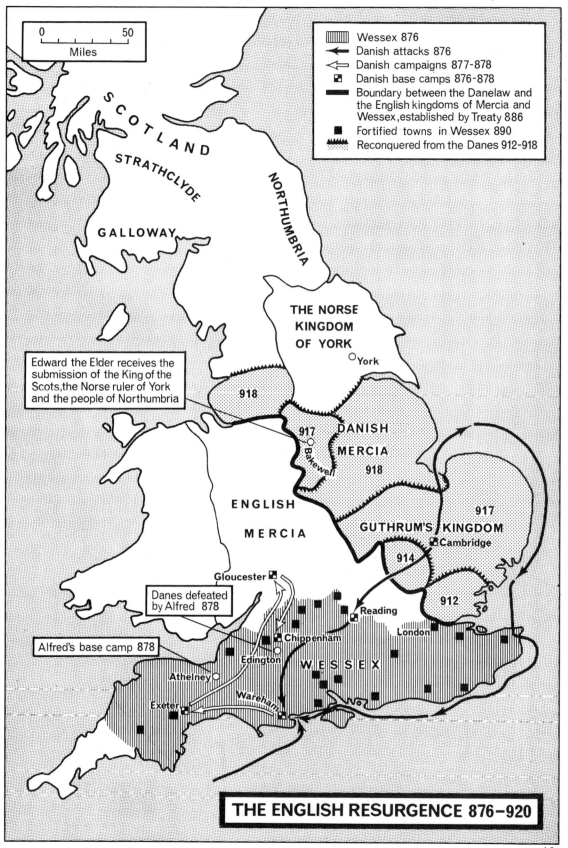

## Map legend

- Wessex 876
- Danish attacks 876
- Danish campaigns 877-878
- Danish base camps 876-878
- Boundary between the Danelaw and the English kingdoms of Mercia and Wessex, established by Treaty 886
- Fortified towns in Wessex 890
- Reconquered from the Danes 912-918

0 — 50 Miles

SCOTLAND

STRATHCLYDE

GALLOWAY

NORTHUMBRIA

THE NORSE KINGDOM OF YORK

York

Edward the Elder receives the submission of the King of the Scots, the Norse ruler of York and the people of Northumbria

918

917
Bakewell

DANISH MERCIA

918

ENGLISH MERCIA

GUTHRUM'S KINGDOM

917

914

Cambridge

912

Gloucester

Danes defeated by Alfred 878

Reading

London

Alfred's base camp 878

Chippenham

Edington

WESSEX

Athelney

Exeter

Wareham

## THE ENGLISH RESURGENCE 876-920

12

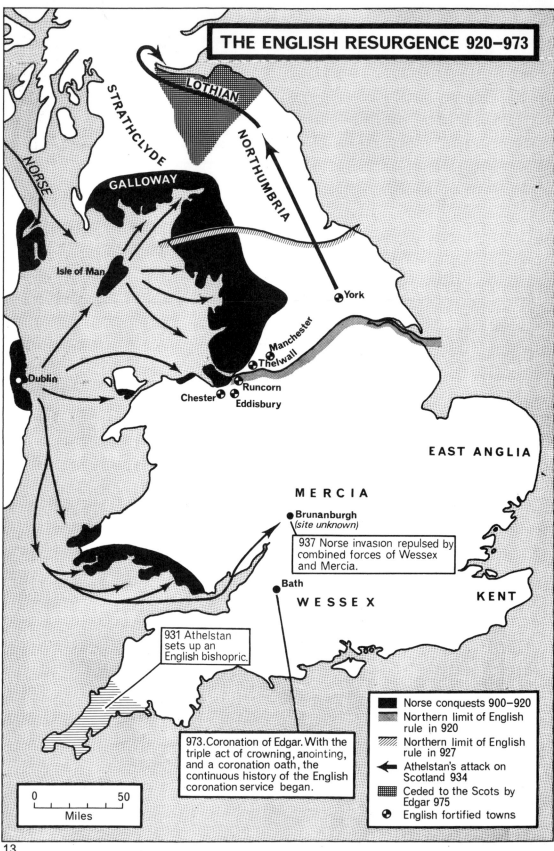

# THE ENGLISH RESURGENCE 920–973

STRATHCLYDE

NORSE

LOTHIAN

GALLOWAY

NORTHUMBRIA

Isle of Man

York

Dublin

Manchester

Thelwall

Runcorn

Chester

Eddisbury

EAST ANGLIA

MERCIA

Brunanburgh
(site unknown)

937 Norse invasion repulsed by
combined forces of Wessex
and Mercia.

Bath

WESSEX

KENT

931 Athelstan
sets up an
English bishopric.

973. Coronation of Edgar. With the
triple act of crowning, anointing,
and a coronation oath, the
continuous history of the English
coronation service began.

0       50
Miles

Norse conquests 900–920

Northern limit of English
rule in 920

Northern limit of English
rule in 927

Athelstan's attack on
Scotland 934

Ceded to the Scots by
Edgar 975

English fortified towns

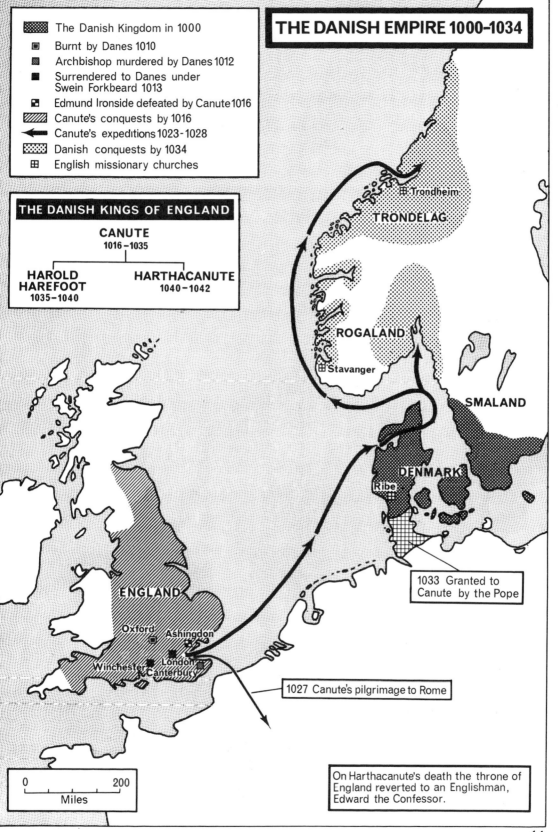

# THE DANISH EMPIRE 1000-1034

**Legend:**
- The Danish Kingdom in 1000
- Burnt by Danes 1010
- Archbishop murdered by Danes 1012
- Surrendered to Danes under Swein Forkbeard 1013
- Edmund Ironside defeated by Canute 1016
- Canute's conquests by 1016
- Canute's expeditions 1023-1028
- Danish conquests by 1034
- English missionary churches

## THE DANISH KINGS OF ENGLAND

**CANUTE**
1016–1035

**HAROLD HAREFOOT**
1035–1040

**HARTHACANUTE**
1040–1042

Trondheim
TRØNDELAG
ROGALAND
Stavanger
SMALAND
DENMARK
Ribe

1033 Granted to Canute by the Pope

ENGLAND
Oxford  Ashingdon
Winchester  London
Canterbury

1027 Canute's pilgrimage to Rome

On Harthacanute's death the throne of England reverted to an Englishman, Edward the Confessor.

0    200
Miles

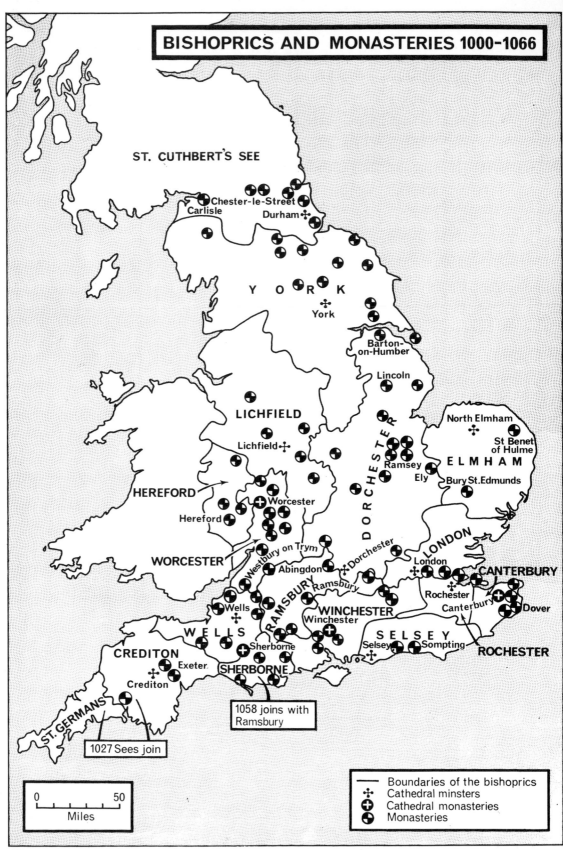

# BISHOPRICS AND MONASTERIES 1000-1066

ST. CUTHBERT'S SEE

Chester-le-Street
Carlisle
Durham

Y O R K

York

Barton-on-Humber

Lincoln

LICHFIELD

North Elmham

St Benet of Hulme

Lichfield

E L M H A M

HEREFORD

Worcester

Ramsey

Ely

Bury St. Edmunds

Hereford

WORCESTER

D O R C H E S T E R

Westbury on Trym

Abingdon

Dorchester

LONDON

London

Ramsbury

Rochester

CANTERBURY

Wells

R A M S B U R Y

WINCHESTER

Winchester

Canterbury

Dover

CREDITON

W E L L S

Sherborne

S E L S E Y

Selsey

Sompting

ROCHESTER

Exeter

SHERBORNE

Crediton

1058 joins with Ramsbury

ST. GERMANS

1027 Sees join

| 0 | 50 |
|---|---|

Miles

—— Boundaries of the bishoprics
✚ Cathedral minsters
✚ Cathedral monasteries
✚ Monasteries

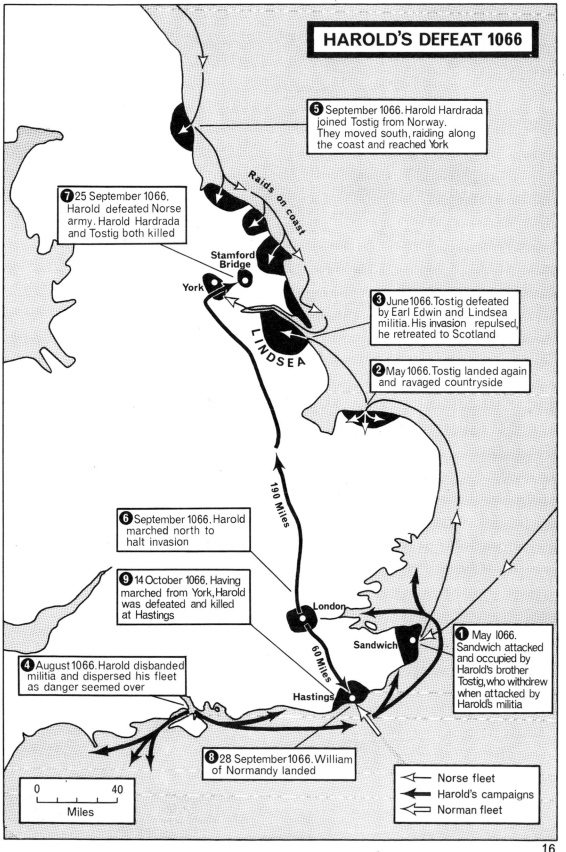

# HAROLD'S DEFEAT 1066

**5** September 1066. Harold Hardrada joined Tostig from Norway. They moved south, raiding along the coast and reached York

**7** 25 September 1066. Harold defeated Norse army. Harold Hardrada and Tostig both killed

Raids on coast

Stamford Bridge

York

LINDSEA

**3** June 1066. Tostig defeated by Earl Edwin and Lindsea militia. His invasion repulsed, he retreated to Scotland

**2** May 1066. Tostig landed again and ravaged countryside

190 Miles

**6** September 1066. Harold marched north to halt invasion

**9** 14 October 1066. Having marched from York, Harold was defeated and killed at Hastings

London

60 Miles

Sandwich

**1** May 1066. Sandwich attacked and occupied by Harold's brother Tostig, who withdrew when attacked by Harold's militia

**4** August 1066. Harold disbanded militia and dispersed his fleet as danger seemed over

Hastings

**8** 28 September 1066. William of Normandy landed

0      40

Miles

⟨ Norse fleet
← Harold's campaigns
⟨ Norman fleet

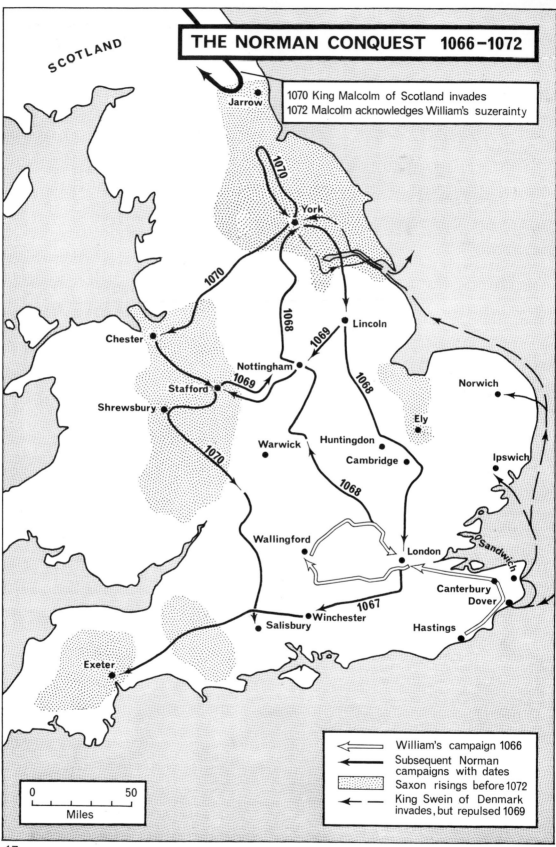

# THE NORMAN CONQUEST 1066-1072

1070 King Malcolm of Scotland invades
1072 Malcolm acknowledges William's suzerainty

SCOTLAND

Jarrow

1070

York

1070

1068

1069

Lincoln

Chester

Nottingham

1069

Stafford

Norwich

Shrewsbury

1068

Ely

1070

Warwick

Huntingdon

Ipswich

Cambridge

1068

Wallingford

London

Sandwich

Canterbury
Dover

1067

Salisbury

Winchester

Hastings

Exeter

0        50
Miles

William's campaign 1066

Subsequent Norman
campaigns with dates

Saxon risings before 1072

King Swein of Denmark
invades, but repulsed 1069

17

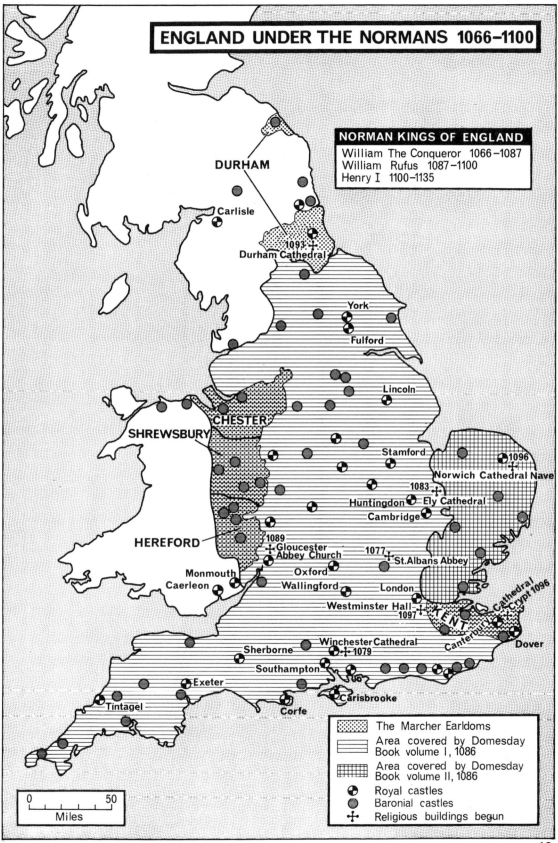

# ENGLAND UNDER THE NORMANS 1066–1100

## NORMAN KINGS OF ENGLAND

William The Conqueror 1066–1087
William Rufus 1087–1100
Henry I 1100–1135

**DURHAM**

Carlisle

1093
Durham Cathedral

York

Fulford

Lincoln

**CHESTER**

**SHREWSBURY**

Stamford

1096
Norwich Cathedral Nave

1083
Huntingdon    Ely Cathedral

Cambridge

**HEREFORD**

1089
Gloucester
Abbey Church    1077
St. Albans Abbey

Monmouth    Oxford
Caerleon    Wallingford    London

Westminster Hall
1097    **KENT**    Canterbury Cathedral Crypt 1096

Winchester Cathedral    Dover
Sherborne    1079

Southampton

Exeter    Carisbrooke

Tintagel    Corfe

| | The Marcher Earldoms |
| --- | --- |
| | Area covered by Domesday Book volume I, 1086 |
| | Area covered by Domesday Book volume II, 1086 |
| | Royal castles |
| | Baronial castles |
| | Religious buildings begun |

0    50
Miles

18

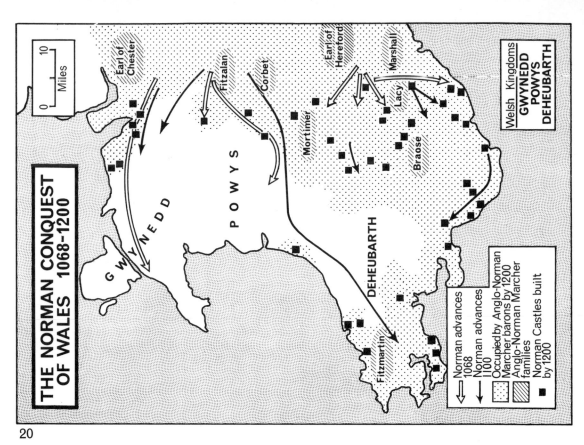

# THE NORMAN CONQUEST OF WALES 1068–1200

Earl of Chester

Fitzalan

Corbet

Earl of Hereford

Marshall

Mortimer

Lacy

Braose

G W Y N E D D

P O W Y S

DEHEUBARTH

Fitzmartin

Welsh Kingdoms
GWYNEDD
POWYS
DEHEUBARTH

Norman advances 1068

Norman advances 1100

Occupied by Anglo-Norman Marcher barons by 1200

Anglo-Norman Marcher families

Norman Castles built by 1200

0 ___ 10
Miles

20

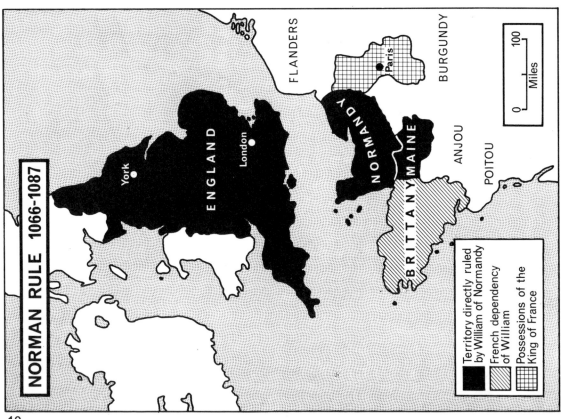

# NORMAN RULE 1066–1087

FLANDERS

Paris

BURGUNDY

ENGLAND

York

London

NORMANDY

BRITTANY

MAINE

ANJOU

POITOU

Territory directly ruled by William of Normandy

French dependency of William

Possessions of the King of France

0 ___ 100
Miles

19

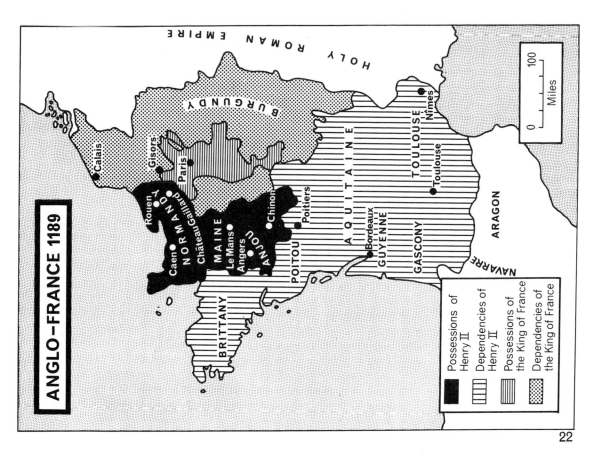

# ANGLO–FRANCE 1189

HOLY ROMAN EMPIRE

BURGUNDY

Calais
Gisors
Rouen
Paris
Château Gaillard
NORMANDY
Caen
MAINE
Le Mans
Angers
ANJOU
Chinon
BRITTANY
POITOU
Poitiers
AQUITAINE
Bordeaux
GUYENNE
GASCONY
TOULOUSE
Toulouse
Nîmes
NAVARRE
ARAGON

Possessions of Henry II

Dependencies of Henry II

Possessions of the King of France

Dependencies of the King of France

0    100
Miles

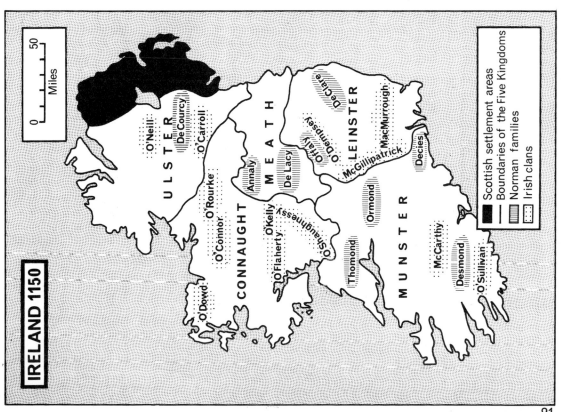

# IRELAND 1150

ULSTER
O'Neill
De Courcy
O'Carroll
O'Rourke
O'Connor
O'Dowd
CONNAUGHT
O'Flaherty
O'Shaughnessy
O'Kelly
Annaly
De Lacy
MEATH
Offaly
O'Dempsey
McGillipatrick
Thomond
Ormond
MUNSTER
McCarthy
Desmond
O'Sullivan
Decies
Decies
MacMurrough
LEINSTER

Scottish settlement areas

Boundaries of the Five Kingdoms

Norman families

Irish clans

0    50
Miles

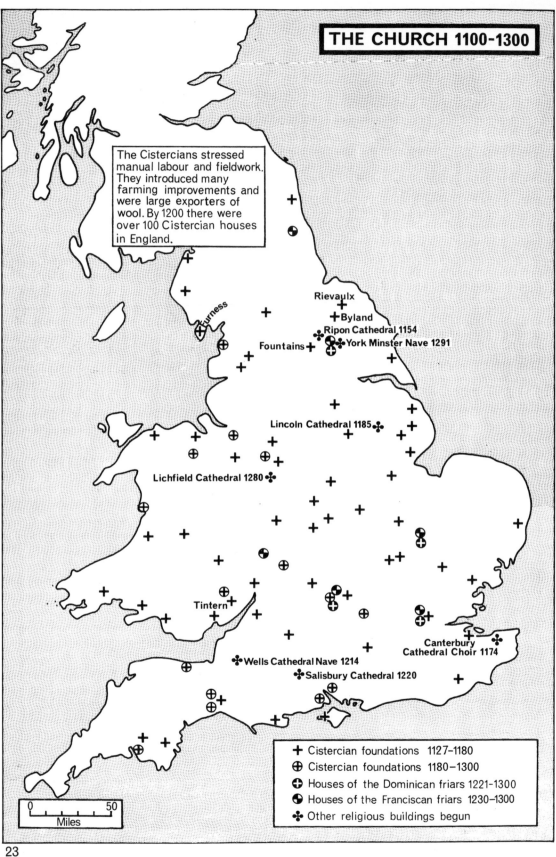

THE CHURCH 1100-1300

The Cistercians stressed manual labour and fieldwork. They introduced many farming improvements and were large exporters of wool. By 1200 there were over 100 Cistercian houses in England.

Furness

Rievaulx
Byland
Ripon Cathedral 1154
Fountains
York Minster Nave 1291

Lincoln Cathedral 1185

Lichfield Cathedral 1280

Tintern

Canterbury
Cathedral Choir 1174

Wells Cathedral Nave 1214
Salisbury Cathedral 1220

✠ Cistercian foundations  1127-1180
⊕ Cistercian foundations  1180-1300
Houses of the Dominican friars 1221-1300
Houses of the Franciscan friars 1230-1300
✤ Other religious buildings begun

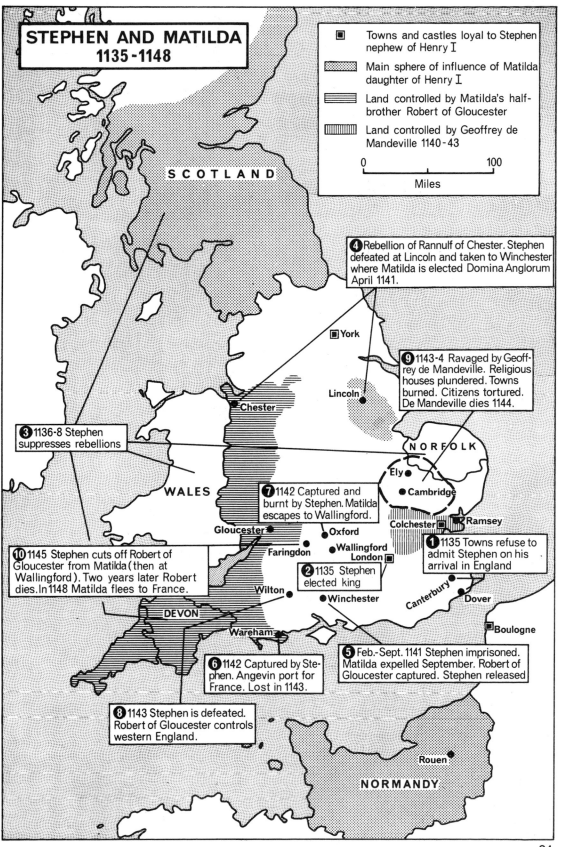

# STEPHEN AND MATILDA
## 1135-1148

**Legend:**

- ■ Towns and castles loyal to Stephen nephew of Henry I
- Main sphere of influence of Matilda daughter of Henry I
- Land controlled by Matilda's half-brother Robert of Gloucester
- Land controlled by Geoffrey de Mandeville 1140-43

0 ——— 100
Miles

SCOTLAND

**4** Rebellion of Rannulf of Chester. Stephen defeated at Lincoln and taken to Winchester where Matilda is elected Domina Anglorum April 1141.

**9** 1143-4 Ravaged by Geoffrey de Mandeville. Religious houses plundered. Towns burned. Citizens tortured. De Mandeville dies 1144.

■ York

Lincoln

NORFOLK

**3** 1136-8 Stephen suppresses rebellions

Chester

Ely
Cambridge

WALES

**7** 1142 Captured and burnt by Stephen. Matilda escapes to Wallingford.

Colchester ■ ■ Ramsey

Gloucester
Oxford
Faringdon
Wallingford
London ■

**1** 1135 Towns refuse to admit Stephen on his arrival in England

**10** 1145 Stephen cuts off Robert of Gloucester from Matilda (then at Wallingford). Two years later Robert dies. In 1148 Matilda flees to France.

**2** 1135 Stephen elected king

Wilton
Winchester
Canterbury
Dover

DEVON

Wareham

Boulogne ■

**6** 1142 Captured by Stephen. Angevin port for France. Lost in 1143.

**5** Feb.-Sept. 1141 Stephen imprisoned. Matilda expelled September. Robert of Gloucester captured. Stephen released

**8** 1143 Stephen is defeated. Robert of Gloucester controls western England.

Rouen

NORMANDY

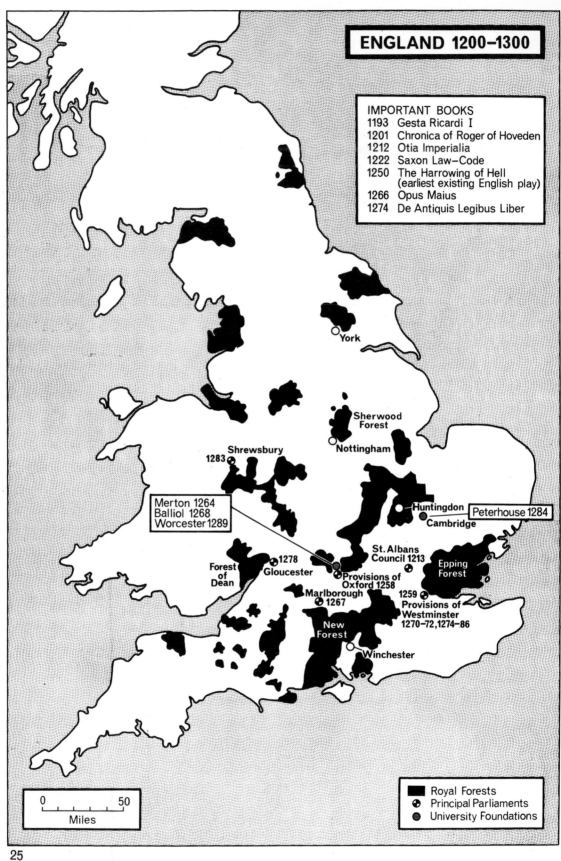

## ENGLAND 1200–1300

**IMPORTANT BOOKS**
1193 Gesta Ricardi I
1201 Chronica of Roger of Hoveden
1212 Otia Imperialia
1222 Saxon Law–Code
1250 The Harrowing of Hell
(earliest existing English play)
1266 Opus Maius
1274 De Antiquis Legibus Liber

York

Sherwood
Forest
Nottingham

Shrewsbury
1283

Merton 1264
Balliol 1268
Worcester 1289

Huntingdon
Cambridge

Peterhouse 1284

St. Albans
Council 1213

Epping
Forest

1278
Gloucester

Forest
of
Dean

Provisions of
Oxford 1258

Marlborough
1267

1259
Provisions of
Westminster
1270–72, 1274–86

New
Forest

Winchester

0        50
Miles

■ Royal Forests
✪ Principal Parliaments
⊜ University Foundations

# THE ECONOMY 1200–1300

1245 Papal money-raiser expelled from England
by king, clergy and barons
1274 Anglo-Flanders Commercial Treaty
1275 King to receive duty on wool
1280 German merchants in England form a Hansa
1290 Expulsion of the Jews from England
1299 Act to repress bad coinage passed

York
blues
Beverley

Lincoln scarlets

Lincoln

Nottingham
Stamfords

Norwich

Leicester
Stamford

Somersham
Ramsey
Coventry
Huntingdon
Northampton
Bury St.Edmunds
Worcester
Cambridge
Warwick
Ipswich
Bedford
Sudbury
Gloucester
russets
russets
Colchester
Chepstow
Oxford
russets
Bristol
Wallingford
London
Marlborough
Canterbury
Sandwich
Devizes
Hythe
Dover
russets
Romney
Wilton
Winchester
Rye
Winchelsea
Salisbury
Hastings

Cloth producing areas with names of cloth
Towns with weavers guilds by 1200
The Cinque Ports: special liberties granted 1278
The liberties of Chepstow, Ramsey and Somersham
Towns with Jewish settlements where Jewish
loans were recorded 1190–1290

0    50
Miles

26

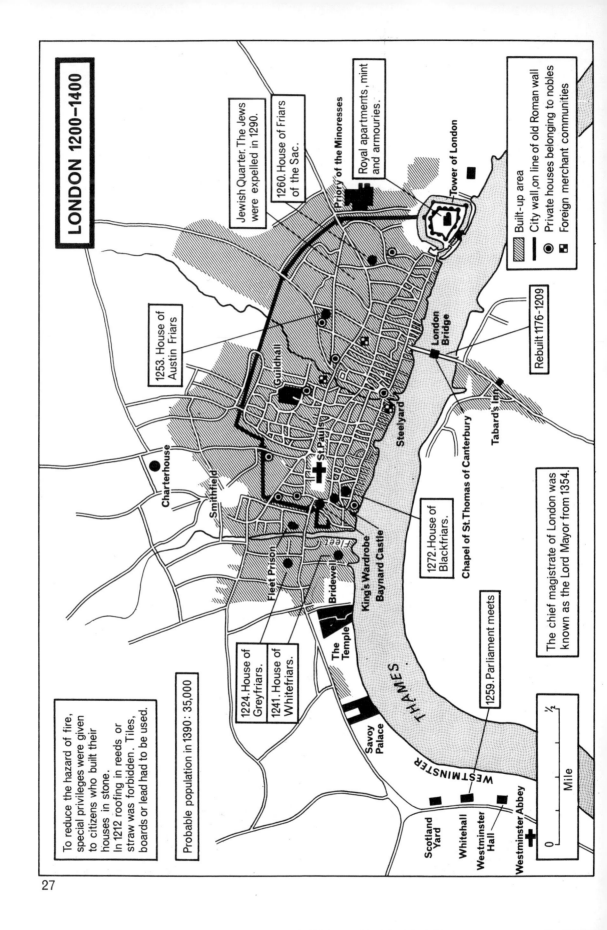

LONDON 1200–1400

Jewish Quarter. The Jews were expelled in 1290.

1260. House of Friars of the Sac.

Royal apartments, mint and armouries.

Priory of the Minoresses

Tower of London

Built-up area

City wall, on line of old Roman wall

Private houses belonging to nobles

Foreign merchant communities

1253. House of Austin Friars

London Bridge

Rebuilt 1176–1209

Guildhall

Steelyard

St. Paul's

Charterhouse

Smithfield

Fleet

1272. House of Blackfriars.

Chapel of St. Thomas of Canterbury

Tabard's Inn

The chief magistrate of London was known as the Lord Mayor from 1354.

Fleet Prison

Bridewell

King's Wardrobe
Baynard Castle

1224. House of Greyfriars.

1241. House of Whitefriars.

The Temple

1259. Parliament meets

Savoy Palace

THAMES.

To reduce the hazard of fire, special privileges were given to citizens who built their houses in stone.
In 1212 roofing in reeds or straw was forbidden. Tiles, boards or lead had to be used.

Probable population in 1390 : 35,000

WESTMINSTER

Scotland Yard

Whitehall

Westminster Hall

Westminster Abbey

0        Mile        ½

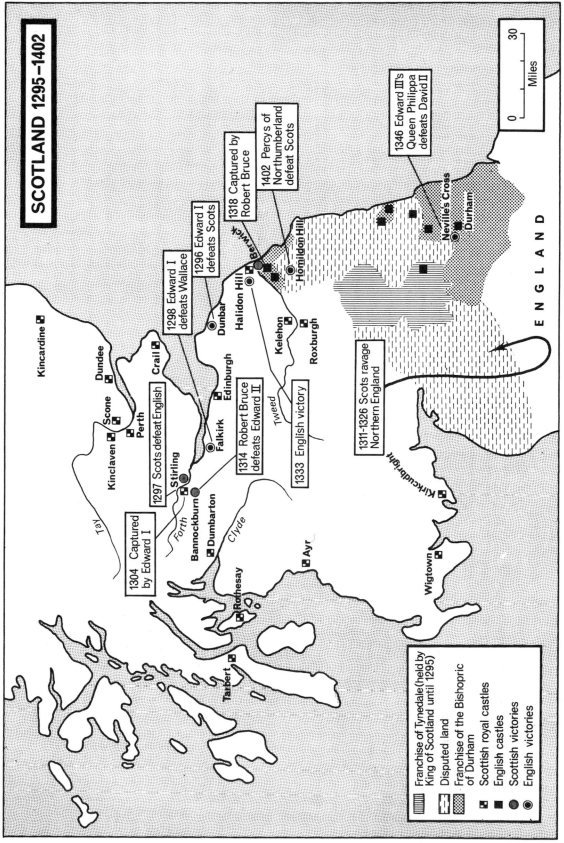

SCOTLAND 1295–1402

1346 Edward III's Queen Philippa defeats David II

1402 Percys of Northumberland defeat Scots

1318 Captured by Robert Bruce

1296 Edward I defeats Scots

1298 Edward I defeats Wallace

1304 Captured by Edward I

1297 Scots defeat English

1314 Robert Bruce defeats Edward II

1333 English victory

1311-1326 Scots ravage Northern England

Neville's Cross

Durham

Homildon Hill

Berwick

Dunbar

Halidon Hill

Kelehon

Roxburgh

Edinburgh

Falkirk

Stirling

Bannockburn

Dumbarton

Forth

Clyde

Tweed

Tay

Kincardine

Dundee

Crail

Scone

Perth

Kinclaven

Ayr

Kirkcudbright

Wigtown

Rothesay

Tarbert

ENGLAND

Miles

0    30

Franchise of Tynedale (held by King of Scotland until 1295)

Disputed land

Franchise of the Bishopric of Durham

Scottish royal castles

English castles

Scottish victories

English victories

c

28

# THE HUNDRED YEARS' WAR
## 1259-1368

0        100
Miles

Calais
Etaples
Crécy
Abbeville

HOLY

Barfleur
Rouen
Caen
NORMANDY
Paris

ROMAN

Bretigny

EMPIRE

F
R
A
N
C
E

ANJOU    Tours
Bourges

Poitiers
POITOU

AQUITAINE

DAUPHINÉ

Bordeaux
GUYENNE

QUERCY
ROUERGUE

GASCONY

Bayonne

Toulouse

Vitoria

Narbonne

Pass of
Roncesvalles
To Burgos   Pamplona
NAVARRE

ARAGON

| | |
|---|---|
| ■ Possessions of Henry III, 1259 | ⇨ Edward III's campaign 1346-1349 |
| · Possessions of the King of France, 1259 | the three campaigns of Edward the Black Prince: |
| ▨ English gains 1275 | → to Narbonne 1355 |
| ▨ English gains at the Treaty of Bretigny, 1368 | ⇢ to Poitiers 1356 |
| | ⇠ to Burgos 1367 |

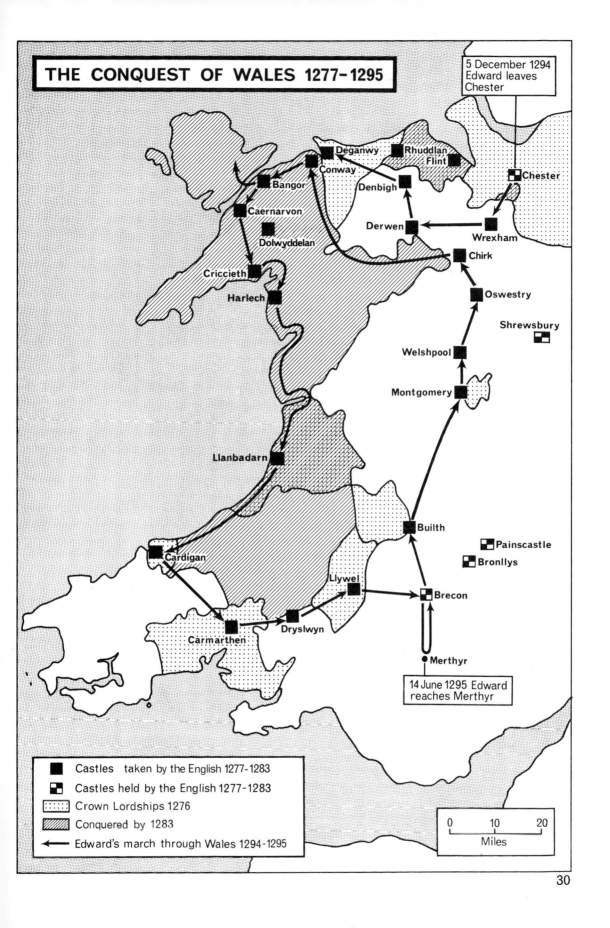

# THE CONQUEST OF WALES 1277-1295

5 December 1294
Edward leaves
Chester

Deganwy
Rhuddlan
Flint
Conway
Chester
Bangor
Denbigh
Caernarvon
Derwen
Wrexham
Dolwyddelan
Chirk
Criccieth
Oswestry
Harlech
Shrewsbury
Welshpool
Montgomery
Llanbadarn
Builth
Painscastle
Cardigan
Bronllys
Llywel
Brecon
Dryslwyn
Carmarthen
Merthyr

14 June 1295 Edward
reaches Merthyr

■ Castles taken by the English 1277-1283

◧ Castles held by the English 1277-1283

∷ Crown Lordships 1276

▨ Conquered by 1283

← Edward's march through Wales 1294-1295

0    10    20
Miles

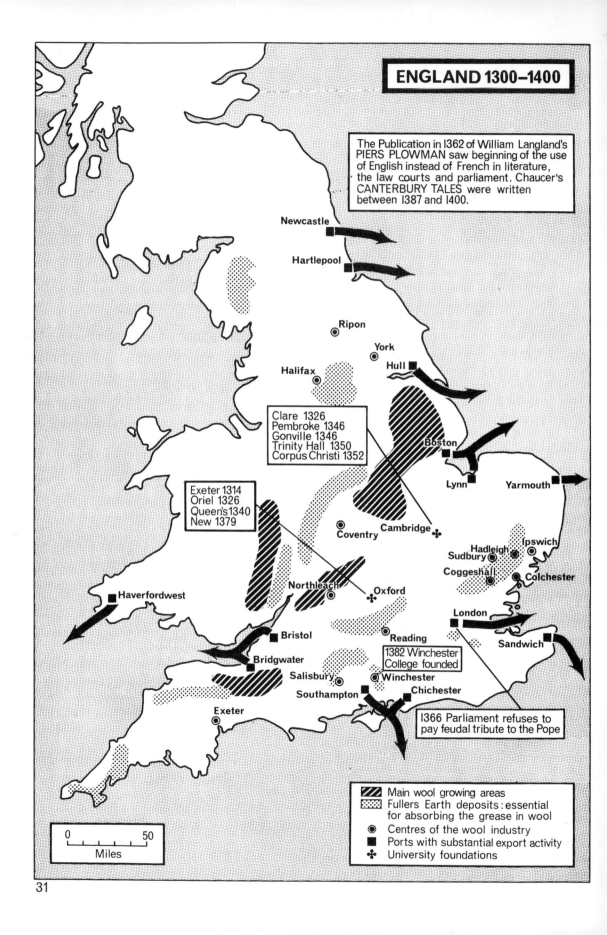

# ENGLAND 1300–1400

The Publication in 1362 of William Langland's PIERS PLOWMAN saw beginning of the use of English instead of French in literature, the law courts and parliament. Chaucer's CANTERBURY TALES were written between 1387 and 1400.

Newcastle

Hartlepool

Ripon

York

Halifax

Hull

Clare 1326
Pembroke 1346
Gonville 1346
Trinity Hall 1350
Corpus Christi 1352

Boston

Exeter 1314
Oriel 1326
Queen's 1340
New 1379

Lynn

Yarmouth

Coventry

Cambridge

Hadleigh
Ipswich
Sudbury
Coggeshall
Colchester

Northleach

Oxford

London

Haverfordwest

Reading

Sandwich

Bristol

1382 Winchester
College founded

Bridgwater

Salisbury

Winchester

Chichester

Southampton

1366 Parliament refuses to
pay feudal tribute to the Pope

Exeter

0    50
Miles

| | Main wool growing areas |
| | Fullers Earth deposits: essential for absorbing the grease in wool |
| ◉ | Centres of the wool industry |
| ■ | Ports with substantial export activity |
| ♣ | University foundations |

31

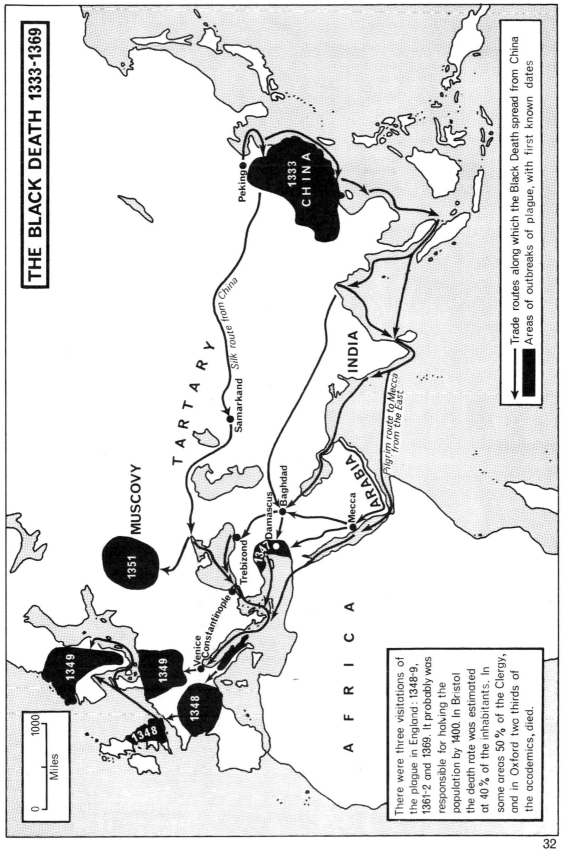

# THE BLACK DEATH 1333-1369

CHINA
1333
Peking

TARTARY

Silk route from China

Samarkand

MUSCOVY
1351

INDIA

Pilgrim route to Mecca
from the East

Baghdad

Damascus
1347

Mecca

ARABIA

Trebizond

Constantinople

Venice
1349

1349

1348

1348

A F R I C A

→ Trade routes along which the Black Death spread from China
■ Areas of outbreaks of plague, with first known dates

1000
Miles
0

There were three visitations of
the plague in England: 1348-9,
1361-2 and 1369. It probably was
responsible for halving the
population by 1400. In Bristol
the death rate was estimated
at 40% of the inhabitants. In
some areas 50% of the Clergy,
and in Oxford two thirds of
the academics, died.

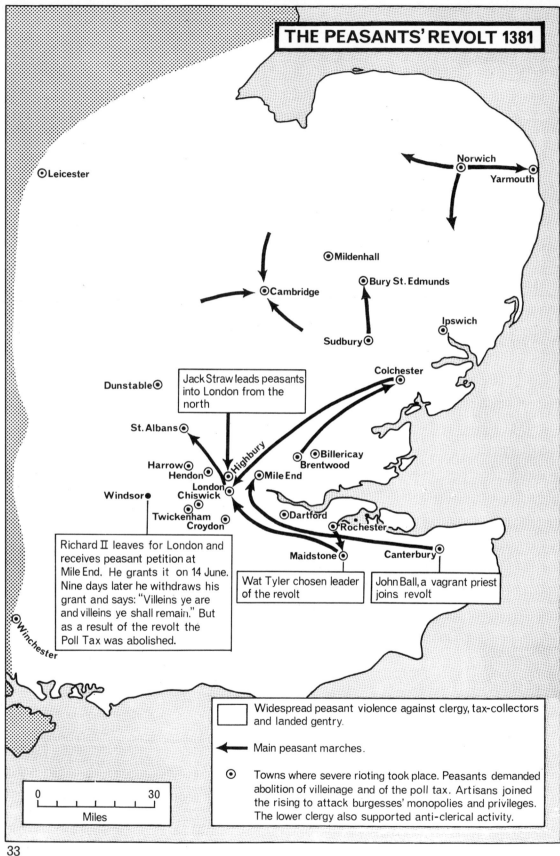

# THE PEASANTS' REVOLT 1381

Leicester

Norwich

Yarmouth

Mildenhall

Bury St. Edmunds

Ipswich

Sudbury

Cambridge

Colchester

Dunstable

Jack Straw leads peasants into London from the north

St. Albans

Highbury

Harrow

Hendon

Billericay

Brentwood

London

Chiswick

Mile End

Windsor

Twickenham

Croydon

Dartford

Rochester

Richard II leaves for London and receives peasant petition at Mile End. He grants it on 14 June. Nine days later he withdraws his grant and says: "Villeins ye are and villeins ye shall remain." But as a result of the revolt the Poll Tax was abolished.

Maidstone

Canterbury

Wat Tyler chosen leader of the revolt

John Ball, a vagrant priest joins revolt

Winchester

Widespread peasant violence against clergy, tax-collectors and landed gentry.

Main peasant marches.

Towns where severe rioting took place. Peasants demanded abolition of villeinage and of the poll tax. Artisans joined the rising to attack burgesses' monopolies and privileges. The lower clergy also supported anti-clerical activity.

0        30
Miles

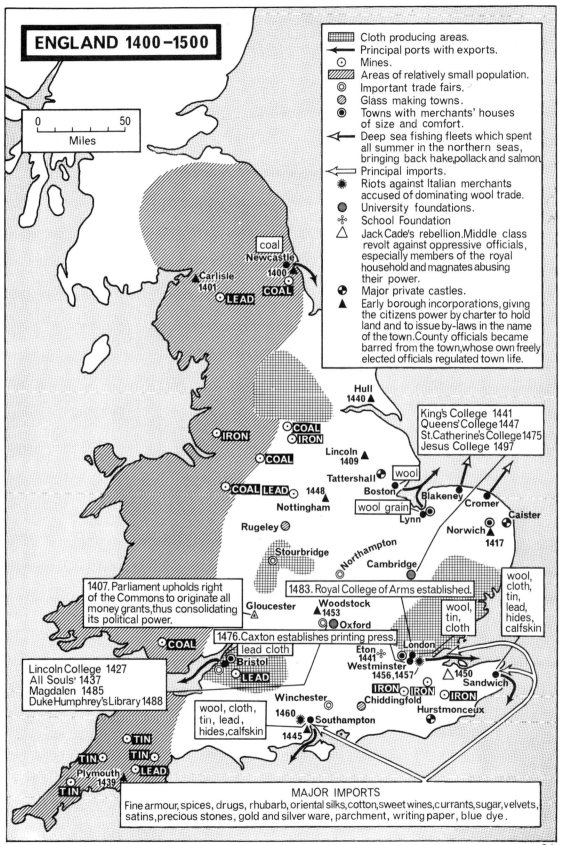

# ENGLAND 1400–1500

**Legend:**
- Cloth producing areas.
- ← Principal ports with exports.
- ⊙ Mines.
- Areas of relatively small population.
- ◎ Important trade fairs.
- ⊘ Glass making towns.
- ◉ Towns with merchants' houses of size and comfort.
- ⇐ Deep sea fishing fleets which spent all summer in the northern seas, bringing back hake, pollack and salmon.
- ⇐ Principal imports.
- ✳ Riots against Italian merchants accused of dominating wool trade.
- ⊜ University foundations.
- ⚘ School Foundation.
- △ Jack Cade's rebellion. Middle class revolt against oppressive officials, especially members of the royal household and magnates abusing their power.
- ◕ Major private castles.
- ▲ Early borough incorporations, giving the citizens power by charter to hold land and to issue by-laws in the name of the town. County officials became barred from the town, whose own freely elected officials regulated town life.

coal
**Newcastle** 1400 **COAL**

**Carlisle** 1401
⊙ **LEAD**

**Hull** 1440 ▲

King's College 1441
Queens' College 1447
St. Catherine's College 1475
Jesus College 1497

⊙ **IRON**
⊙ **COAL**
⊙ **IRON**

⊙ **COAL**

**Lincoln** 1409 ▲

**Tattershall** ✚ wool

⊙ **COAL** **LEAD** ⊙ 1448 ▲
**Nottingham**

**Boston**
wool grain
**Blakeney** **Cromer**
**Lynn**
**Caister**

**Rugeley** ⊘

**Norwich** ◎ ▲ 1417

**Stourbridge** ⊙

**Northampton**

**Cambridge** ◎ ⊜

wool, cloth, tin, lead, hides, calfskin

1483. Royal College of Arms established.

1407. Parliament upholds right of the Commons to originate all money grants, thus consolidating its political power.

**Gloucester** △

**Woodstock** ▲ 1453
◎⊜ **Oxford**

wool, tin, cloth

1476. Caxton establishes printing press.

⊙ **COAL**

Lincoln College 1427
All Souls' 1437
Magdalen 1485
Duke Humphrey's Library 1488

lead cloth
◉ **Bristol**
⊙ **LEAD**

**Eton** ⚘
**Westminster** 1456, 1457

✳ **London**
⊙ **IRON** ⊙ **IRON** ⊙ **IRON**
△ 1450
**Sandwich** ◉

wool, cloth, tin, lead, hides, calfskin

**Winchester** ◎ 1460
✳ ◉ **Southampton**
1445

**Chiddingfold** ⊘
**Hurstmonceux** ◕

⊙ **TIN**
⊙ **TIN**  ⊙ **TIN**
⊙ **TIN** ⊙ **LEAD**
**Plymouth** 1439 ▲

## MAJOR IMPORTS
Fine armour, spices, drugs, rhubarb, oriental silks, cotton, sweet wines, currants, sugar, velvets, satins, precious stones, gold and silver ware, parchment, writing paper, blue dye.

0 ____ 50
Miles

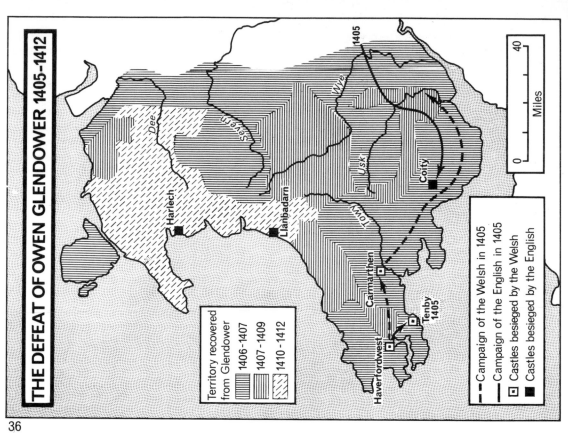

# THE DEFEAT OF OWEN GLENDOWER 1405-1412

Territory recovered from Glendower
- 1406-1407
- 1407-1409
- 1410-1412

- - - Campaign of the Welsh in 1405
—— Campaign of the English in 1405
▢ Castles besieged by the Welsh
■ Castles besieged by the English

Harlech

Llanbadarn

Carmarthen

Haverfordwest

Tenby 1405

Coity

1405

*Wye*

*Severn*

*Usk*

*Towy*

Miles
0        40

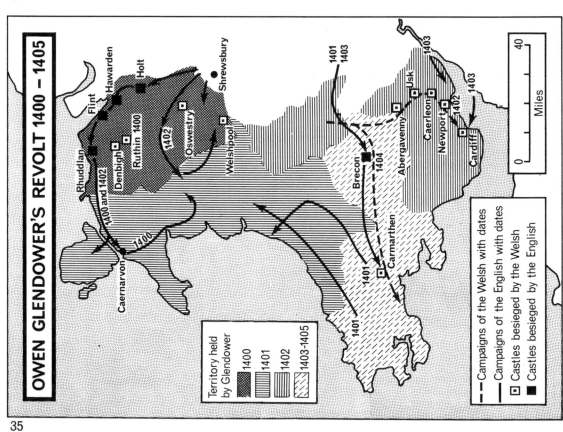

# OWEN GLENDOWER'S REVOLT 1400 – 1405

Territory held by Glendower
- 1400
- 1401
- 1402
- 1403-1405

- - - Campaigns of the Welsh with dates
—— Campaigns of the English with dates
▢ Castles besieged by the Welsh
■ Castles besieged by the English

Flint
Hawarden
Holt
Rhuddlan
Denbigh
Ruthin 1400
Oswestry
Shrewsbury
Welshpool

Caernarvon

1400 and 1402
1400
1402
1401

Brecon
1404
Carmarthen
Abergavenny
Usk
Caerleon
Newport
Cardiff

1401
1403
1401
1402
1403
1403

Miles
0        40

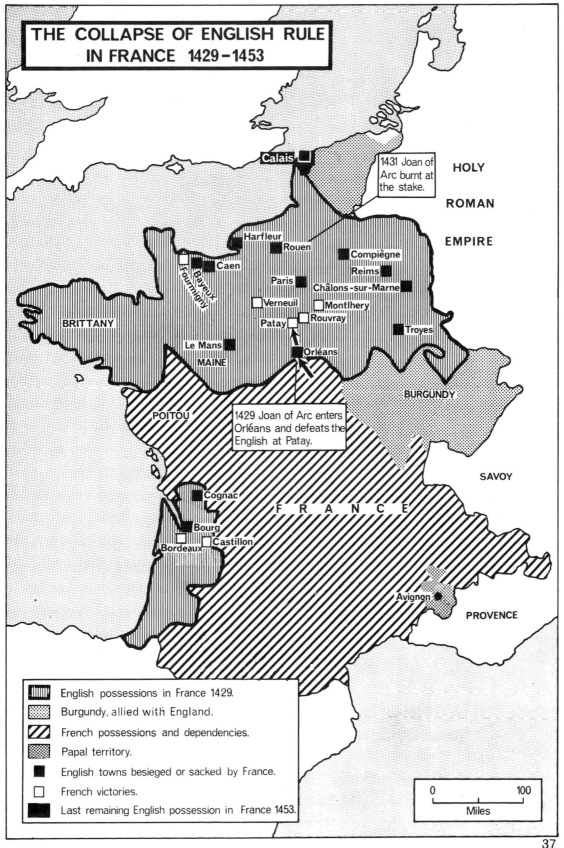

# THE COLLAPSE OF ENGLISH RULE IN FRANCE 1429–1453

HOLY

ROMAN

EMPIRE

Calais

1431 Joan of Arc burnt at the stake.

Harfleur

Rouen

Compiègne

Caen

Bayeux

Fourmigny

Reims

Paris

Châlons-sur-Marne

Verneuil

Montlhery

Patay

Rouvray

BRITTANY

Troyes

Le Mans

Orléans

MAINE

BURGUNDY

1429 Joan of Arc enters Orléans and defeats the English at Patay.

POITOU

SAVOY

Cognac

F R A N C E

Bourg

Castillon

Bordeaux

Avignon

PROVENCE

English possessions in France 1429.

Burgundy, allied with England.

French possessions and dependencies.

Papal territory.

English towns besieged or sacked by France.

French victories.

Last remaining English possession in France 1453.

0        100

Miles

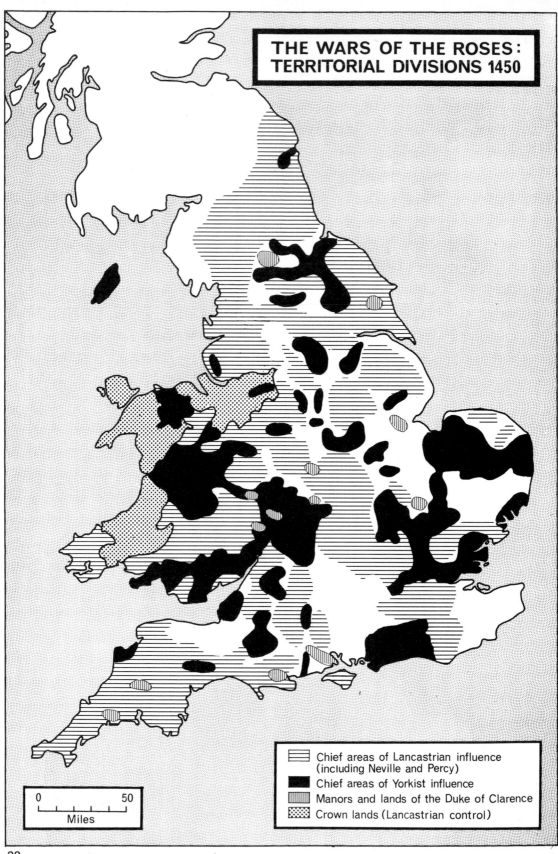

**THE WARS OF THE ROSES: TERRITORIAL DIVISIONS 1450**

Chief areas of Lancastrian influence (including Neville and Percy)

Chief areas of Yorkist influence

Manors and lands of the Duke of Clarence

Crown lands (Lancastrian control)

0 — 50
Miles

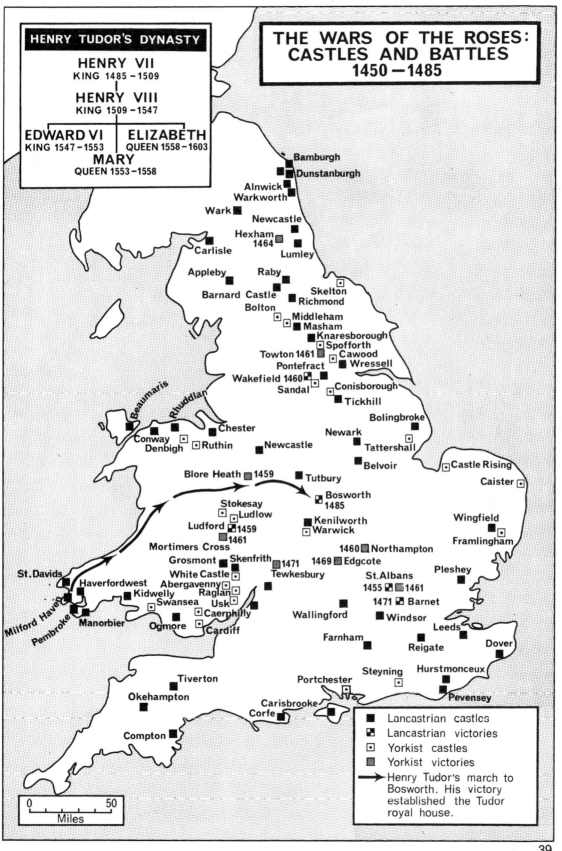

**HENRY TUDOR'S DYNASTY**

HENRY VII
KING 1485–1509

HENRY VIII
KING 1509–1547

EDWARD VI
KING 1547–1553

ELIZABETH
QUEEN 1558–1603

MARY
QUEEN 1553–1558

**THE WARS OF THE ROSES: CASTLES AND BATTLES 1450 – 1485**

Bamburgh
Dunstanburgh
Alnwick
Warkworth
Wark
Newcastle
Hexham 1464
Lumley
Carlisle
Appleby
Raby
Barnard Castle
Skelton
Richmond
Bolton
Middleham
Masham
Knaresborough
Spofforth
Towton 1461
Cawood
Pontefract
Wressell
Wakefield 1460
Sandal
Conisborough
Tickhill
Bolingbroke
Newark
Newcastle
Tattershall
Belvoir
Castle Rising
Caister
Blore Heath 1459
Tutbury
Bosworth 1485
Stokesay
Ludlow
Ludford 1459 1461
Kenilworth
Warwick
Wingfield
Framlingham
Mortimers Cross
Grosmont
Skenfrith 1471
Tewkesbury
1460 Northampton
1469 Edgcote
Pleshey
St. Davids
White Castle
Abergavenny
Raglan
St.Albans 1455 1461
Haverfordwest
Kidwelly
Swansea
Usk
1471 Barnet
Milford Haven
Manorbier
Pembroke
Ogmore
Caerphilly
Cardiff
Wallingford
Windsor
Leeds
Farnham
Reigate
Dover
Tiverton
Steyning
Hurstmonceux
Portchester
Okehampton
Carisbrooke
Corfe
Pevensey
Compton

Beaumaris
Rhuddlan
Conway
Denbigh
Ruthin
Chester

Lancastrian castles
Lancastrian victories
Yorkist castles
Yorkist victories
Henry Tudor's march to Bosworth. His victory established the Tudor royal house.

0    50
Miles

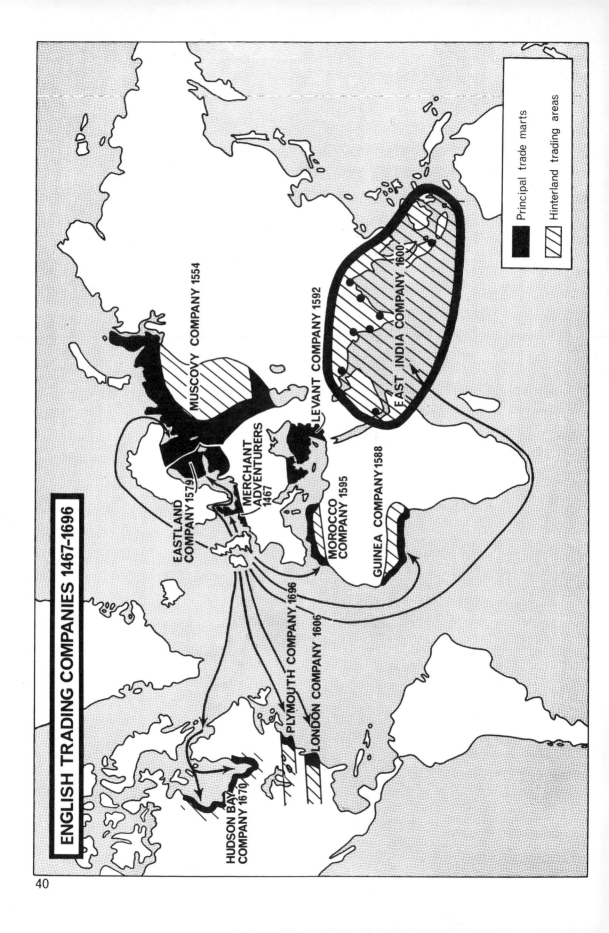

# ENGLISH TRADING COMPANIES 1467-1696

EASTLAND COMPANY 1579

MUSCOVY COMPANY 1554

MERCHANT ADVENTURERS 1467

LEVANT COMPANY 1592

EAST INDIA COMPANY 1600

MOROCCO COMPANY 1595

GUINEA COMPANY 1588

HUDSON BAY COMPANY 1670

PLYMOUTH COMPANY 1696

LONDON COMPANY 1606

Principal trade marts

Hinterland trading areas

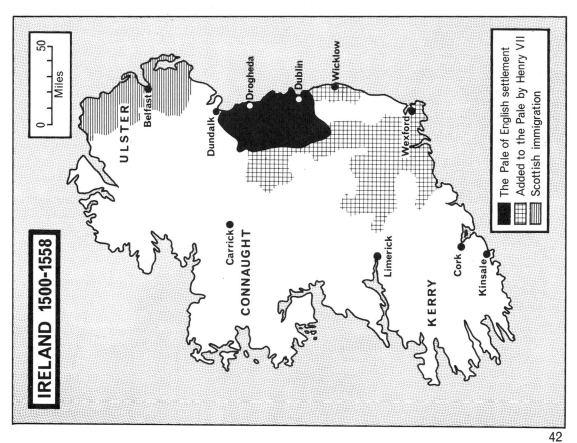

## IRELAND 1500-1558

Legend:
- The Pale of English settlement
- Added to the Pale by Henry VII
- Scottish immigration

ULSTER

Belfast
Dundalk
Drogheda
Dublin
Wicklow
Wexford

Carrick
CONNAUGHT

Limerick

KERRY

Cork
Kinsale

Miles 0 — 50

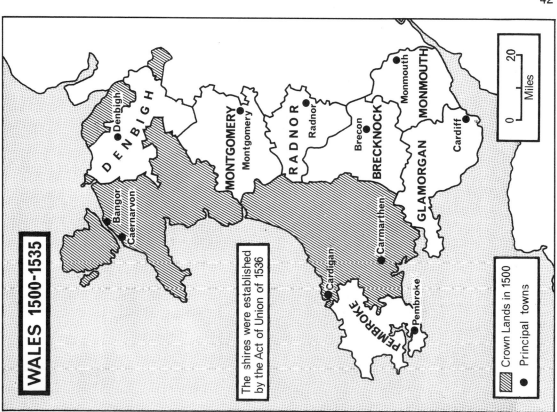

## WALES 1500-1535

The shires were established by the Act of Union of 1536

DENBIGH
Denbigh
Bangor
Caernarvon

MONTGOMERY
Montgomery

RADNOR
Radnor

BRECKNOCK
Brecon

MONMOUTH
Monmouth

GLAMORGAN
Cardiff

Carmarthen
Cardigan

PEMBROKE
Pembroke

Legend:
- Crown Lands in 1500
- Principal towns

Miles 0 — 20

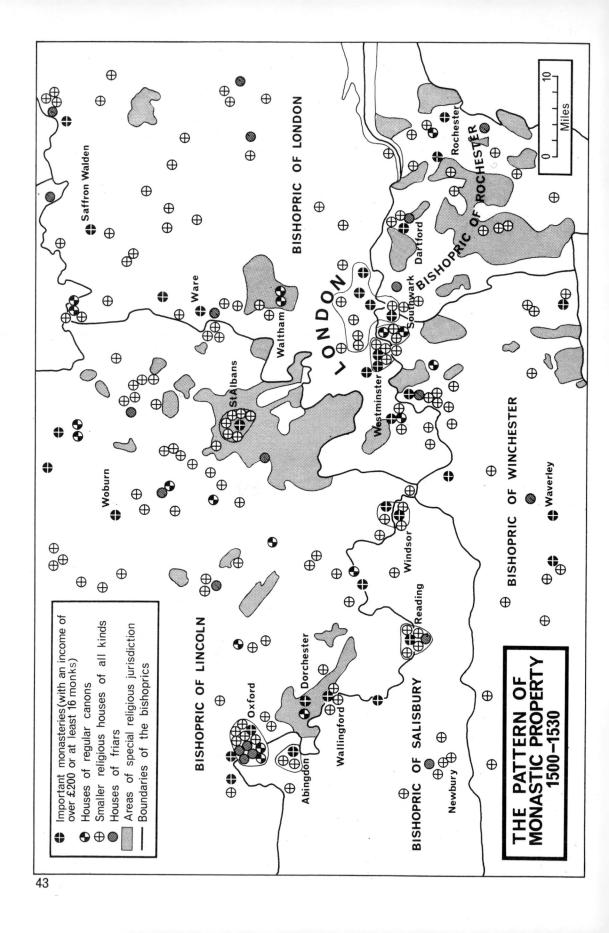

THE PATTERN OF
MONASTIC PROPERTY
1500–1530

BISHOPRIC OF LONDON

BISHOPRIC OF ROCHESTER

BISHOPRIC OF WINCHESTER

BISHOPRIC OF LINCOLN

BISHOPRIC OF SALISBURY

LONDON

Saffron Walden

Ware

Waltham

St Albans

Woburn

Westminster

Southwark

Dartford

Rochester

Waverley

Windsor

Reading

Oxford

Dorchester

Wallingford

Abingdon

Newbury

Important monasteries (with an income of
over £200 or at least 16 monks)

Houses of regular canons

Smaller religious houses of all kinds

Houses of friars

Areas of special religious jurisdiction

Boundaries of the bishoprics

10

0

Miles

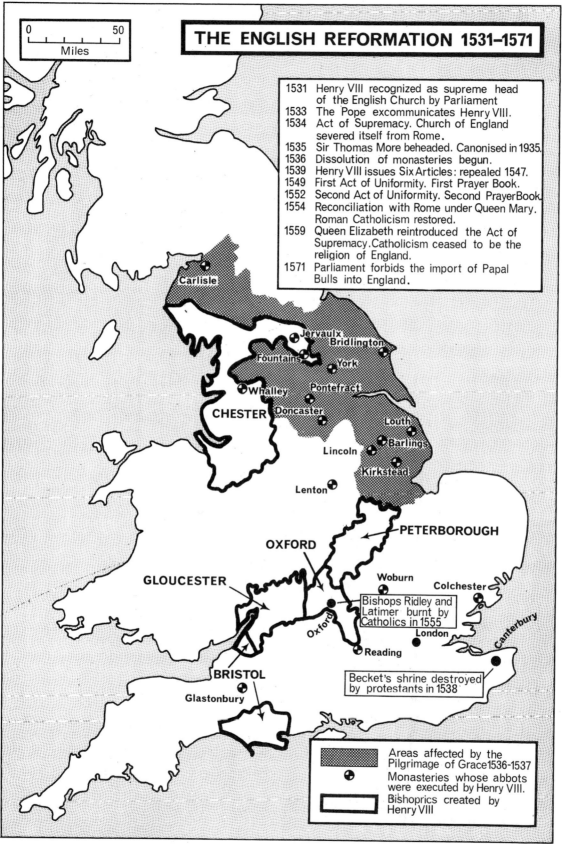

# THE ENGLISH REFORMATION 1531–1571

**Scale:** 0 — 50 Miles

1531 Henry VIII recognized as supreme head of the English Church by Parliament
1533 The Pope excommunicates Henry VIII.
1534 Act of Supremacy. Church of England severed itself from Rome.
1535 Sir Thomas More beheaded. Canonised in 1935.
1536 Dissolution of monasteries begun.
1539 Henry VIII issues Six Articles: repealed 1547.
1549 First Act of Uniformity. First Prayer Book.
1552 Second Act of Uniformity. Second Prayer Book.
1554 Reconciliation with Rome under Queen Mary. Roman Catholicism restored.
1559 Queen Elizabeth reintroduced the Act of Supremacy. Catholicism ceased to be the religion of England.
1571 Parliament forbids the import of Papal Bulls into England.

Carlisle

Jervaulx
Bridlington
Fountains
York
Whalley
Pontefract
CHESTER
Doncaster
Louth
Barlings
Lincoln
Kirkstead
Lenton

PETERBOROUGH

OXFORD

GLOUCESTER

Woburn
Colchester

Bishops Ridley and Latimer burnt by Catholics in 1555

Oxford
London
Canterbury

Reading

BRISTOL

Becket's shrine destroyed by protestants in 1538

Glastonbury

**Legend:**
Areas affected by the Pilgrimage of Grace 1536-1537
Monasteries whose abbots were executed by Henry VIII.
Bishoprics created by Henry VIII

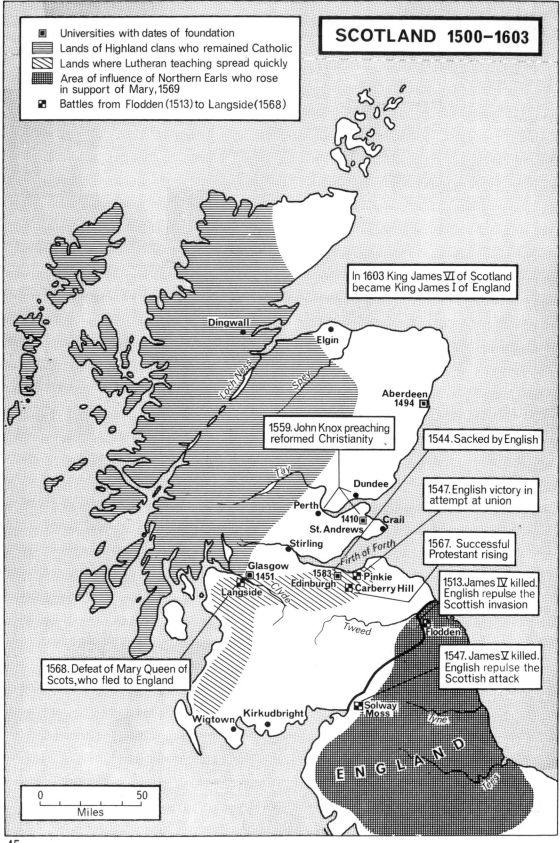

**SCOTLAND 1500–1603**

Universities with dates of foundation

Lands of Highland clans who remained Catholic

Lands where Lutheran teaching spread quickly

Area of influence of Northern Earls who rose in support of Mary, 1569

Battles from Flodden (1513) to Langside (1568)

In 1603 King James VI of Scotland became King James I of England

Dingwall

Elgin

*Loch Ness*

*Spey*

Aberdeen 1494

1559. John Knox preaching reformed Christianity

1544. Sacked by English

*Tay*

Dundee

1547. English victory in attempt at union

Perth

1410 Crail
St. Andrews

1567. Successful Protestant rising

Stirling

Glasgow
1451

1583
Edinburgh

Pinkie

Carberry Hill

1513. James IV killed. English repulse the Scottish invasion

Langside

*Clyde*

*Firth of Forth*

*Tweed*

Flodden

1547. James V killed. English repulse the Scottish attack

1568. Defeat of Mary Queen of Scots, who fled to England

Solway
Moss

*Tyne*

Wigtown

Kirkudbright

E N G L A N D

*Tees*

0        50
Miles

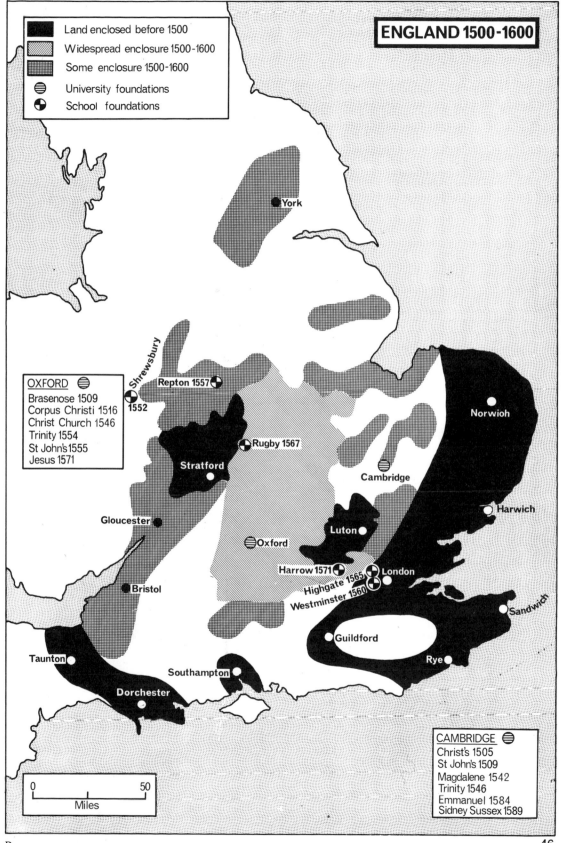

ENGLAND 1500-1600

Land enclosed before 1500
Widespread enclosure 1500-1600
Some enclosure 1500-1600
University foundations
School foundations

OXFORD
Brasenose 1509
Corpus Christi 1516
Christ Church 1546
Trinity 1554
St John's 1555
Jesus 1571

Shrewsbury
1552

Repton 1557

Rugby 1567

Stratford

Gloucester

Oxford

Cambridge

Norwioh

Harwich

Luton

Harrow 1571
Highgate 1565
Westminster 1560

London

Bristol

Taunton

Southampton

Dorchester

Guildford

Rye

Sandwich

0        50
Miles

CAMBRIDGE
Christ's 1505
St John's 1509
Magdalene 1542
Trinity 1546
Emmanuel 1584
Sidney Sussex 1589

York

D

46

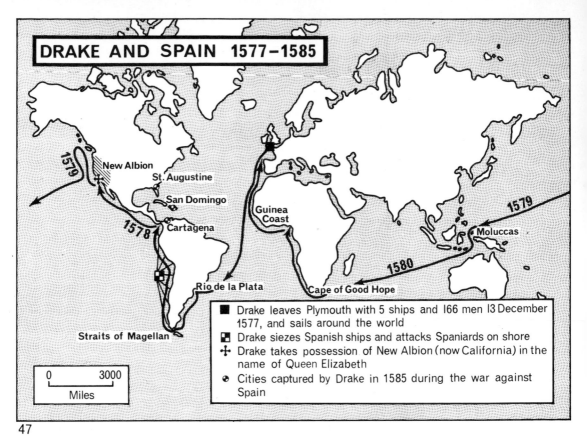

# DRAKE AND SPAIN 1577–1585

New Albion
St. Augustine
San Domingo
Guinea Coast
Cartagena
Moluccas
1579
1578
1580
Rio de la Plata
Cape of Good Hope
Straits of Magellan

■ Drake leaves Plymouth with 5 ships and 166 men 13 December 1577, and sails around the world

▣ Drake siezes Spanish ships and attacks Spaniards on shore

✟ Drake takes possession of New Albion (now California) in the name of Queen Elizabeth

◕ Cities captured by Drake in 1585 during the war against Spain

0    3000
Miles

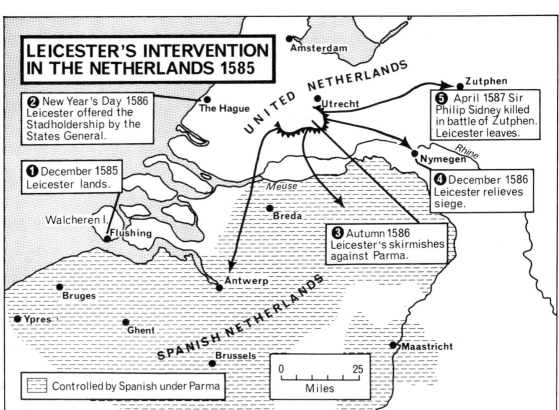

# LEICESTER'S INTERVENTION IN THE NETHERLANDS 1585

Amsterdam

UNITED NETHERLANDS

Zutphen

The Hague

Utrecht

❷ New Year's Day 1586 Leicester offered the Stadholdership by the States General.

❺ April 1587 Sir Philip Sidney killed in battle of Zutphen. Leicester leaves.

❶ December 1585 Leicester lands.

Rhine
Nymegen

Meuse

❹ December 1586 Leicester relieves siege.

Walcheren I.
Flushing

Breda

❸ Autumn 1586 Leicester's skirmishes against Parma.

Antwerp

Bruges

SPANISH NETHERLANDS

Ypres

Ghent

Maastricht

Brussels

0    25
Miles

▨ Controlled by Spanish under Parma

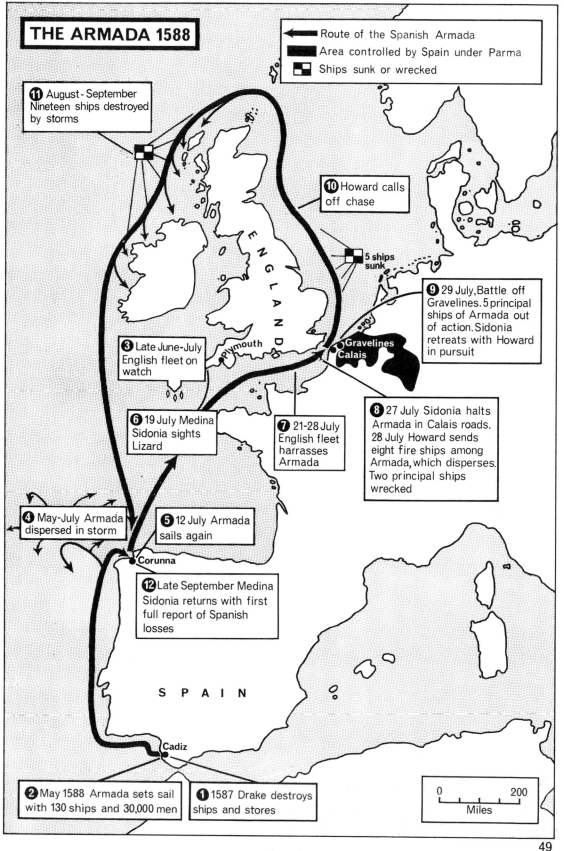

# THE ARMADA 1588

→ Route of the Spanish Armada
■ Area controlled by Spain under Parma
▨ Ships sunk or wrecked

**11** August - September Nineteen ships destroyed by storms

**10** Howard calls off chase

5 ships sunk

**9** 29 July, Battle off Gravelines. 5 principal ships of Armada out of action. Sidonia retreats with Howard in pursuit

**3** Late June-July English fleet on watch

Plymouth

Gravelines
Calais

E N G L A N D

**6** 19 July Medina Sidonia sights Lizard

**7** 21-28 July English fleet harrasses Armada

**8** 27 July Sidonia halts Armada in Calais roads. 28 July Howard sends eight fire ships among Armada, which disperses. Two principal ships wrecked

**4** May-July Armada dispersed in storm

**5** 12 July Armada sails again

Corunna

**12** Late September Medina Sidonia returns with first full report of Spanish losses

S P A I N

Cadiz

**2** May 1588 Armada sets sail with 130 ships and 30,000 men

**1** 1587 Drake destroys ships and stores

0    200
Miles

49

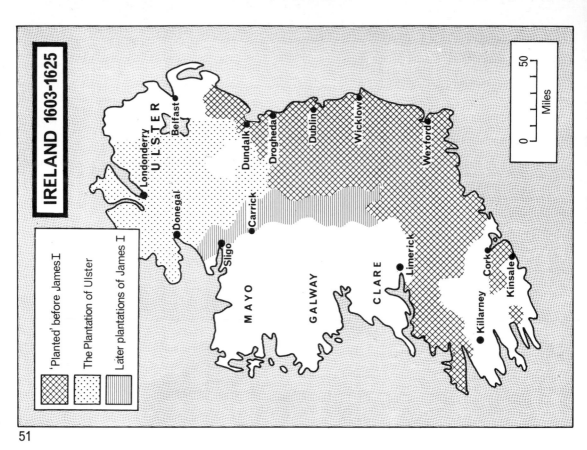

# IRELAND 1603-1625

'Planted' before James I

The Plantation of Ulster

Later plantations of James I

ULSTER

Londonderry
Belfast
Donegal
Dundalk
Carrick
Drogheda
Dublin
Wicklow
Sligo
MAYO
GALWAY
Wexford
CLARE
Limerick
Killarney
Cork
Kinsale

0    50
Miles

51

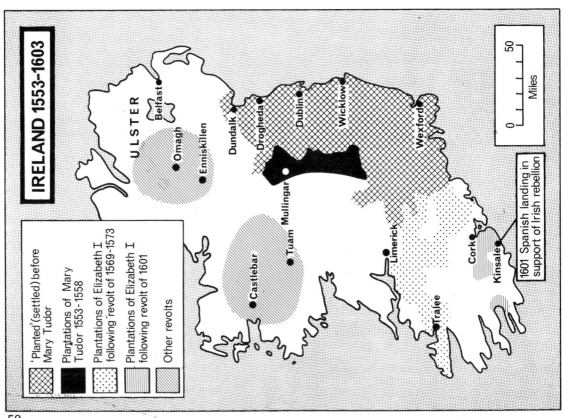

# IRELAND 1553-1603

'Planted' (settled) before
Mary Tudor

Plantations of Mary
Tudor 1553-1558

Plantations of Elizabeth I
following 'revolt of 1569-1573

Plantations of Elizabeth I
following revolt of 1601

Other revolts

ULSTER

Belfast
Omagh
Enniskillen
Dundalk
Drogheda
Dublin
Wicklow
Castlebar
Mullingar
Tuam
Wexford
Limerick
Tralee
Cork
Kinsale

1601 Spanish landing in
support of Irish rebellion

0    50
Miles

50

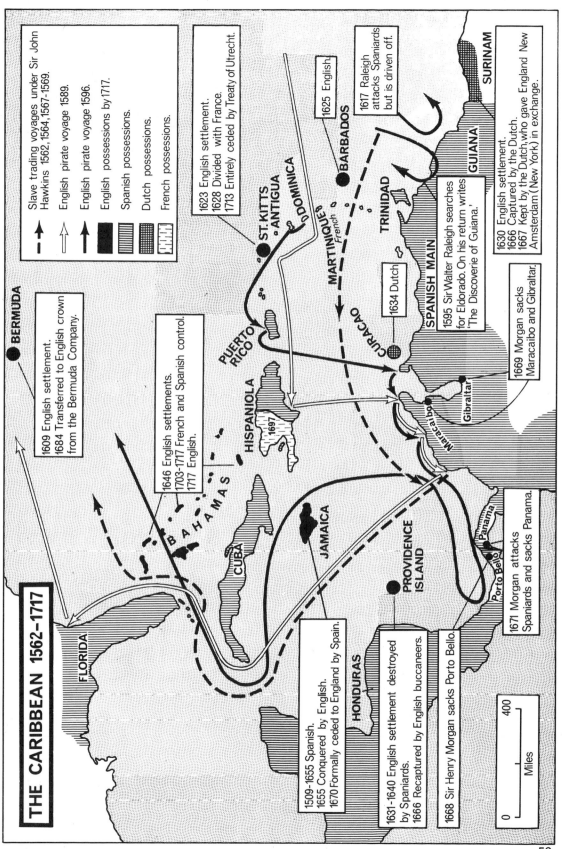

# THE CARIBBEAN 1562–1717

**Key**

→ Slave trading voyages under Sir John Hawkins 1562, 1564, 1567-1569.

⇧ English pirate voyage 1589.

⬆ English pirate voyage 1596.

■ English possessions by 1717.

▥ Spanish possessions.

▦ Dutch possessions.

▨ French possessions.

**BERMUDA**
1609 English settlement.
1684 Transferred to English crown from the Bermuda Company.

**ST. KITTS · ANTIGUA**
1623 English settlement.
1628 Divided with France.
1713 Entirely ceded by Treaty of Utrecht.

**DOMINICA**

**BARBADOS**
1625 English.

**SURINAM**

**GUIANA**
1617 Raleigh attacks Spaniards but is driven off.

1630 English settlement.
1666 Captured by the Dutch.
1667 Kept by the Dutch, who gave England New Amsterdam (New York) in exchange.

**MARTINIQUE**
French

**TRINIDAD**

**CURACAO**
1634 Dutch

**SPANISH MAIN**
1595 Sir Walter Raleigh searches for Eldorado. On his return writes 'The Discoverie of Guiana.'

**PUERTO RICO**

**HISPANIOLA**
1697
1646 English settlements.
1703-1717 French and Spanish control.
1717 English.

**BAHAMAS**

**CUBA**

**JAMAICA**

**PROVIDENCE ISLAND**
1631-1640 English settlement destroyed by Spaniards.
1666 Recaptured by English buccaneers.

**FLORIDA**

**HONDURAS**
1509-1655 Spanish.
1655 Conquered by English.
1670 Formally ceded to England by Spain.

**Maracaibo**

**Gibraltar**
1669 Morgan sacks Maracaibo and Gibraltar.

**Panama**
1671 Morgan attacks Spaniards and sacks Panama.

**Porto Bello**
1668 Sir Henry Morgan sacks Porto Bello.

0 ___ 400
Miles

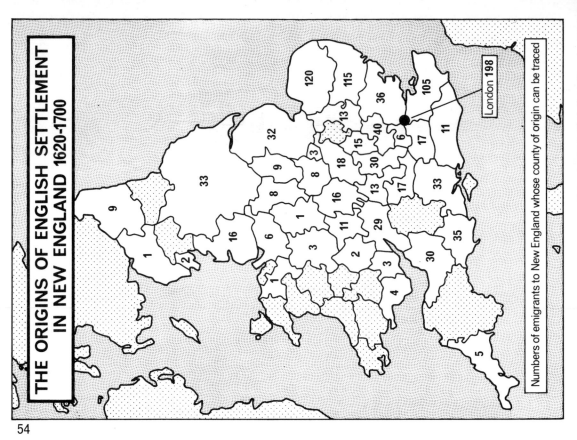

## THE ORIGINS OF ENGLISH SETTLEMENT IN NEW ENGLAND 1620-1700

London 198

Numbers of emigrants to New England whose county of origin can be traced

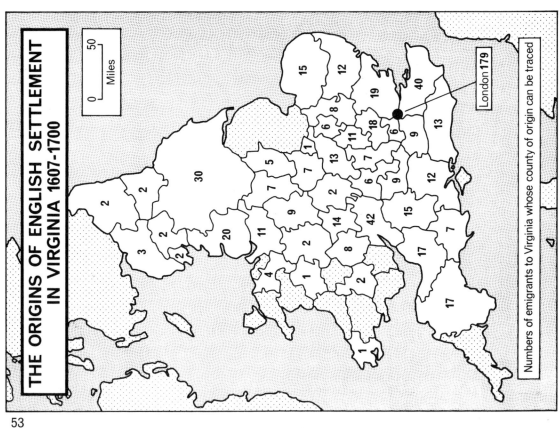

## THE ORIGINS OF ENGLISH SETTLEMENT IN VIRGINIA 1607-1700

0    50
Miles

London 179

Numbers of emigrants to Virginia whose county of origin can be traced

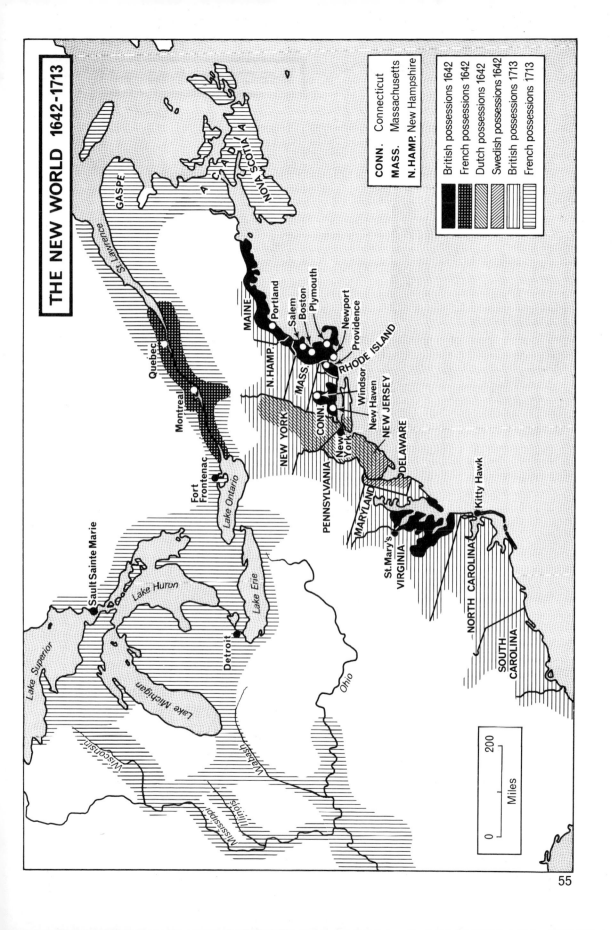

# THE NEW WORLD 1642-1713

| CONN. | Connecticut |
|---|---|
| MASS. | Massachusetts |
| N. HAMP. | New Hampshire |

British possessions 1642
French possessions 1642
Dutch possessions 1642
Swedish possessions 1642
British possessions 1713
French possessions 1713

GASPE

NOVA SCOTIA

St. Lawrence

Quebec

Montreal

Fort Frontenac

Lake Ontario

Sault Sainte Marie

Lake Superior

Lake Huron

Lake Michigan

Lake Erie

Detroit

Wisconsin

Mississippi

Illinois

Wabash

Ohio

MAINE

Portland

Salem
Boston
Plymouth

Newport
Providence

N. HAMP.

MASS.

RHODE ISLAND

CONN.

Windsor

New Haven

New York

NEW JERSEY

NEW YORK

PENNSYLVANIA

DELAWARE

MARYLAND

St. Mary's

VIRGINIA

Kitty Hawk

NORTH CAROLINA

SOUTH CAROLINA

0   200

Miles

55

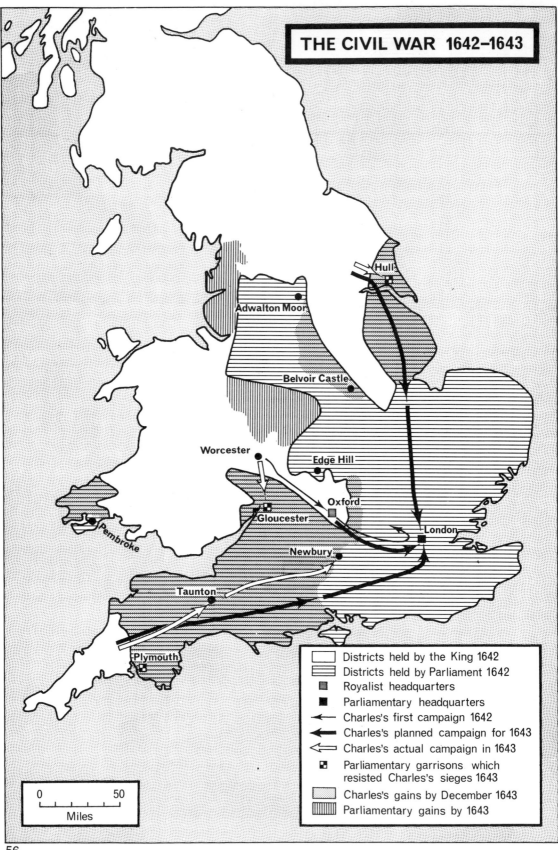

## THE CIVIL WAR 1642–1643

Hull

Adwalton Moor

Belvoir Castle

Worcester

Edge Hill

Oxford

Gloucester

Pembroke

London

Newbury

Taunton

Plymouth

Districts held by the King 1642

Districts held by Parliament 1642

Royalist headquarters

Parliamentary headquarters

Charles's first campaign 1642

Charles's planned campaign for 1643

Charles's actual campaign in 1643

Parliamentary garrisons which resisted Charles's sieges 1643

Charles's gains by December 1643

Parliamentary gains by 1643

0        50
Miles

# THE CIVIL WAR 1644–1646

In May 1646 King Charles surrendered to the Scottish Army at Newark. In February 1647 the Scots sold the King to Parliament for £400,000. He was beheaded on 30 January 1649.

Carlisle

Marston Moor

Hull

Preston
Bolton

Liverpool

Stockport

Sandal Castle

Hulme

Nantwich

Newark

Shrewsbury

Belvoir Castle

Ashby

Lichfield

Naseby

Holmby House

Banbury
Cropredy Bridge

Gloucester

Oxford

Donnington Castle

Bridgewater

Taunton

Lyme
Regis

Corfe Castle

Plymouth

The Eastern Association: main recruiting ground for Parliamentary Army 1643

Campaign of Prince Rupert to Marston Moor.

Parliamentary advances to Marston Moor, where the Royalists were defeated 2 July 1644

Area controlled by Parliament in December 1644.

Area gained by Parliament by December 1645.

Districts held by the King in May 1646.

Area gained by Parliament by December 1646.

0        50
Miles

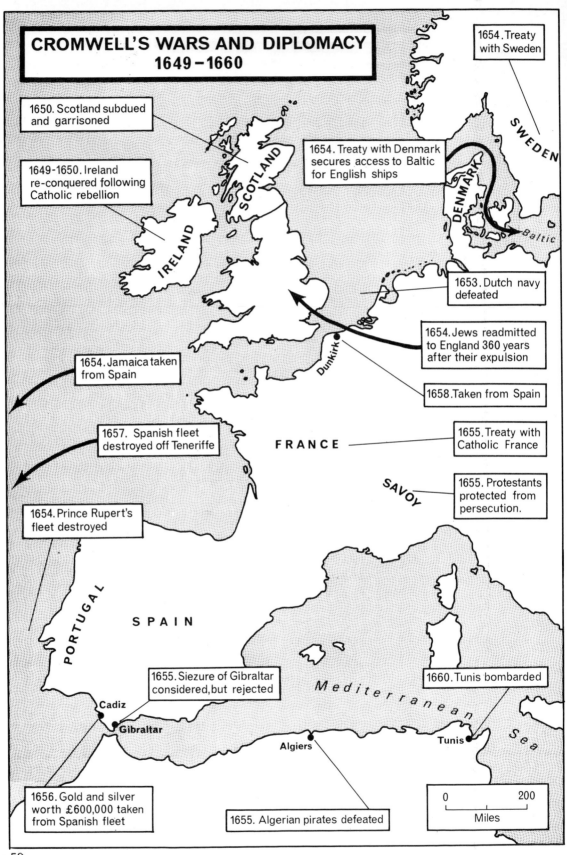

# CROMWELL'S WARS AND DIPLOMACY 1649–1660

1654. Treaty with Sweden

1650. Scotland subdued and garrisoned

1654. Treaty with Denmark secures access to Baltic for English ships

1649–1650. Ireland re-conquered following Catholic rebellion

1653. Dutch navy defeated

1654. Jamaica taken from Spain

1654. Jews readmitted to England 360 years after their expulsion

1658. Taken from Spain

1657. Spanish fleet destroyed off Teneriffe

1655. Treaty with Catholic France

1655. Protestants protected from persecution.

1654. Prince Rupert's fleet destroyed

1655. Siezure of Gibraltar considered, but rejected

1660. Tunis bombarded

1656. Gold and silver worth £600,000 taken from Spanish fleet

1655. Algerian pirates defeated

SWEDEN

DENMARK

Baltic

SCOTLAND

IRELAND

Dunkirk

FRANCE

SAVOY

PORTUGAL

SPAIN

Cadiz

Gibraltar

Algiers

Tunis

Mediterranean Sea

0      200
Miles

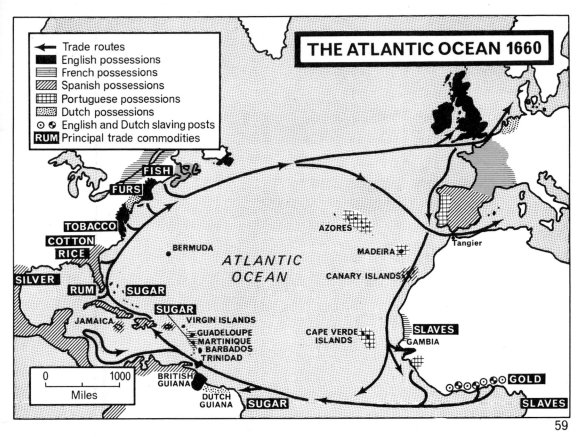

## THE ATLANTIC OCEAN 1660

**Legend:**
- → Trade routes
- ■ English possessions
- ▤ French possessions
- ▨ Spanish possessions
- ▦ Portuguese possessions
- ░ Dutch possessions
- ⊙ ◑ English and Dutch slaving posts
- **RUM** Principal trade commodities

FISH

FURS

TOBACCO

COTTON

RICE

SILVER

RUM

SUGAR

BERMUDA

ATLANTIC OCEAN

AZORES

MADEIRA

Tangier

CANARY ISLANDS

SUGAR

JAMAICA

VIRGIN ISLANDS

GUADELOUPE

MARTINIQUE

BARBADOS

TRINIDAD

CAPE VERDE ISLANDS

SLAVES

GAMBIA

0 — 1000

Miles

BRITISH GUIANA

DUTCH GUIANA

SUGAR

GOLD

SLAVES

59

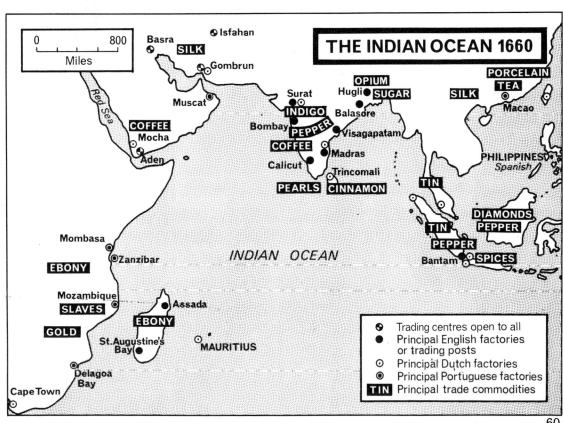

## THE INDIAN OCEAN 1660

0 — 800

Miles

Basra

Isfahan

SILK

Gombrun

Muscat

Surat

Hugli

OPIUM

SUGAR

PORCELAIN

TEA

SILK

Macao

INDIGO

Balasore

Bombay

PEPPER

Visagapatam

COFFEE

Mocha

COFFEE

Madras

Calicut

Trincomali

PHILIPPINES
*Spanish*

Aden

PEARLS

CINNAMON

TIN

Red Sea

DIAMONDS

PEPPER

TIN

PEPPER

Mombasa

INDIAN OCEAN

Bantam

SPICES

EBONY

Zanzibar

Mozambique

SLAVES

GOLD

Assada

EBONY

St.Augustine's Bay

MAURITIUS

Delagoa Bay

Cape Town

**Legend:**
- ◍ Trading centres open to all
- ● Principal English factories or trading posts
- ⊙ Principal Dutch factories
- ◉ Principal Portuguese factories
- **TIN** Principal trade commodities

60

# THE THREE DUTCH WARS

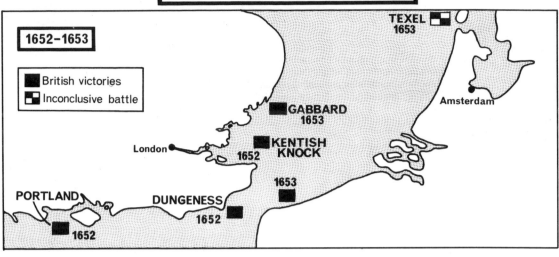

**1652-1653**

- ■ British victories
- ◱ Inconclusive battle

TEXEL 1653

GABBARD 1653

London

KENTISH KNOCK 1652

PORTLAND 1652

DUNGENESS 1652

1653

Amsterdam

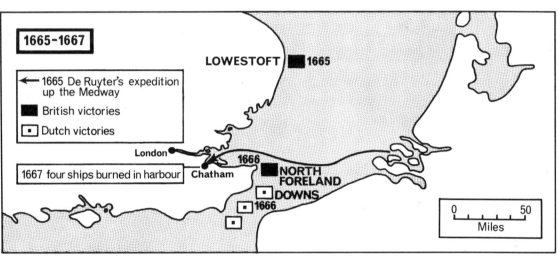

**1665-1667**

- ← 1665 De Ruyter's expedition up the Medway
- ■ British victories
- ▣ Dutch victories

LOWESTOFT ■1665

London

1667 four ships burned in harbour

Chatham

1666

NORTH FORELAND

▣ DOWNS

▣ 1666

0        50
Miles

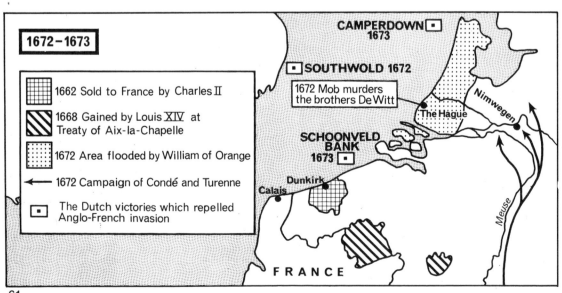

**1672-1673**

- ▦ 1662 Sold to France by Charles II
- ▨ 1668 Gained by Louis XIV at Treaty of Aix-la-Chapelle
- ▦ 1672 Area flooded by William of Orange
- ← 1672 Campaign of Condé and Turenne
- ▣ The Dutch victories which repelled Anglo-French invasion

CAMPERDOWN ▣ 1673

▣ SOUTHWOLD 1672

1672 Mob murders the brothers De Witt

The Hague

Nimwegen

SCHOONVELD BANK 1673 ▣

Dunkirk

Calais

Meuse

F R A N C E

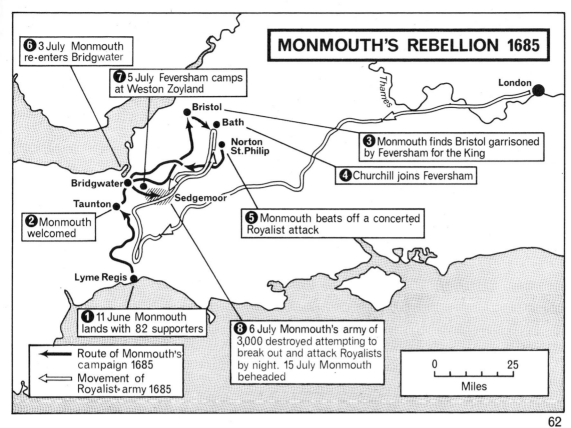

**MONMOUTH'S REBELLION 1685**

❻ 3 July Monmouth re-enters Bridgwater

❼ 5 July Feversham camps at Weston Zoyland

❸ Monmouth finds Bristol garrisoned by Feversham for the King

❹ Churchill joins Feversham

❺ Monmouth beats off a concerted Royalist attack

❷ Monmouth welcomed

❶ 11 June Monmouth lands with 82 supporters

❽ 6 July Monmouth's army of 3,000 destroyed attempting to break out and attack Royalists by night. 15 July Monmouth beheaded

Bristol
Bath
Norton St.Philip
Bridgwater
Sedgemoor
Taunton
Lyme Regis
London
Thames

← Route of Monmouth's campaign 1685
⇐ Movement of Royalist army 1685

0        25
Miles

62

---

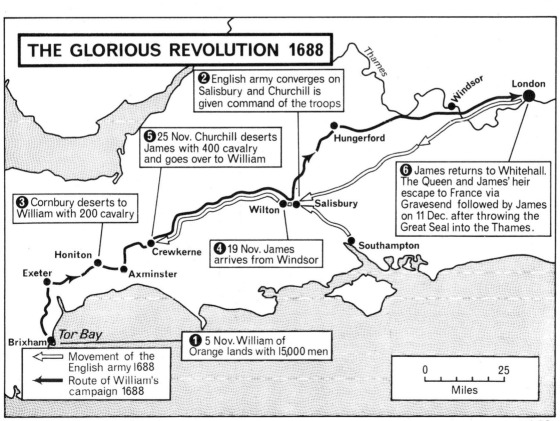

**THE GLORIOUS REVOLUTION 1688**

❷ English army converges on Salisbury and Churchill is given command of the troops

❺ 25 Nov. Churchill deserts James with 400 cavalry and goes over to William

❸ Cornbury deserts to William with 200 cavalry

❻ James returns to Whitehall. The Queen and James' heir escape to France via Gravesend followed by James on 11 Dec. after throwing the Great Seal into the Thames.

❹ 19 Nov. James arrives from Windsor

❶ 5 Nov. William of Orange lands with 15,000 men

Thames
Windsor
London
Hungerford
Wilton
Salisbury
Southampton
Honiton
Crewkerne
Exeter
Axminster
Brixham
*Tor Bay*

⇐ Movement of the English army 1688
← Route of William's campaign 1688

0        25
Miles

63

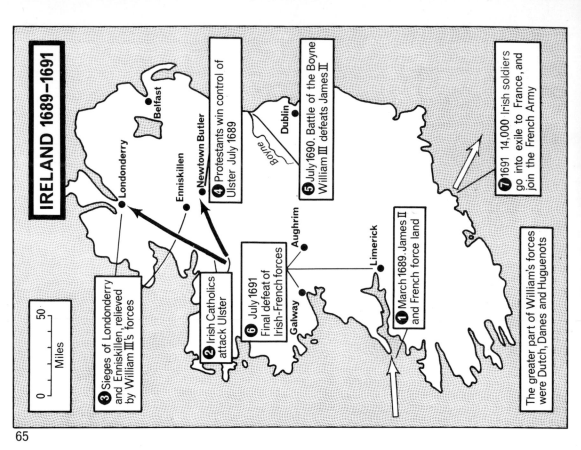

## IRELAND 1689–1691

**3** Sieges of Londonderry and Enniskillen, relieved by William III's forces

**2** Irish Catholics attack Ulster

**6** July 1691 Final defeat of Irish-French forces

**1** March 1689. James II and French force land

**4** Protestants win control of Ulster July 1689

**5** July 1690. Battle of the Boyne William III defeats James II

**7** 1691 14,000 Irish soldiers go into exile to France, and join the French Army

The greater part of William's forces were Dutch, Danes and Huguenots

Belfast
Londonderry
Enniskillen
Newtown Butler
Dublin
Boyne
Aughrim
Limerick
Galway

0 · · · · 50
Miles

65

---

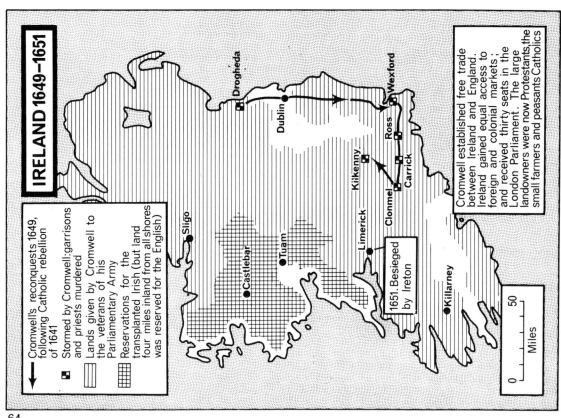

## IRELAND 1649–1651

Cromwell's reconquests 1649, following Catholic rebellion of 1641

■ Stormed by Cromwell: garrisons and priests murdered

|||  Lands given by Cromwell to the veterans of his Parliamentary Army

▦  Reservations for the transplanted Irish (but land four miles inland from all shores was reserved for the English)

Cromwell established free trade between Ireland and England. Ireland gained equal access to foreign and colonial markets; and received thirty seats in the London Parliament. The large landowners were now Protestants, the small farmers and peasants Catholics

Drogheda
Dublin
Wexford
Ross
Carrick
Clonmel
Kilkenny
Limerick
Sligo
Castlebar
Tuam
Killarney

1651. Besieged by Ireton

0 · · · · 50
Miles

64

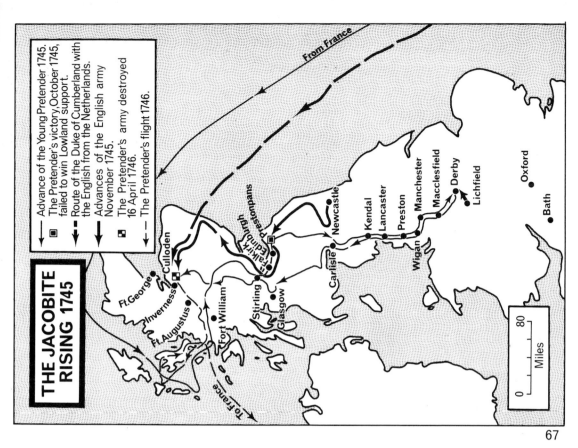

## THE JACOBITE RISING 1745

Advance of the Young Pretender 1745.
The Pretender's victory, October 1745, failed to win Lowland support.
Route of the Duke of Cumberland with the English from the Netherlands.
Advances of the English army November 1745.
The Pretender's army destroyed 16 April 1746.
The Pretender's flight 1746.

From France

Culloden
Ft.George
Inverness
Ft.Augustus
Fort William
Stirling
Glasgow
Edinburgh
Falkirk
Prestonpans
Carlisle
Newcastle
Kendal
Lancaster
Preston
Wigan
Manchester
Macclesfield
Derby
Lichfield
Oxford
Bath

To France

0    80
Miles

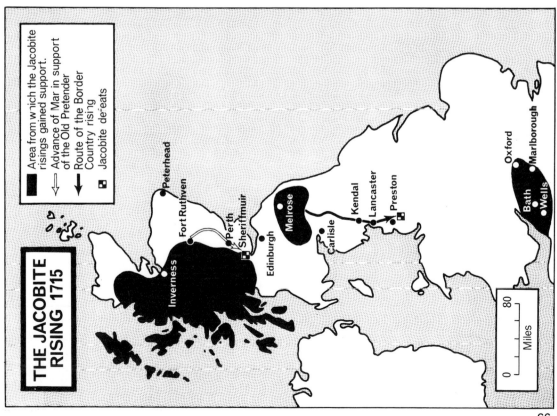

## THE JACOBITE RISING 1715

Area from wich the Jacobite risings gained support.
Advance of Mar in support of the Old Pretender
Route of the Border Country rising
Jacobite defeats

Peterhead
Fort Ruthven
Inverness
Perth
Sheriffmuir
Edinburgh
Melrose
Carlisle
Kendal
Lancaster
Preston
Oxford
Marlborough
Bath
Wells

0    80
Miles

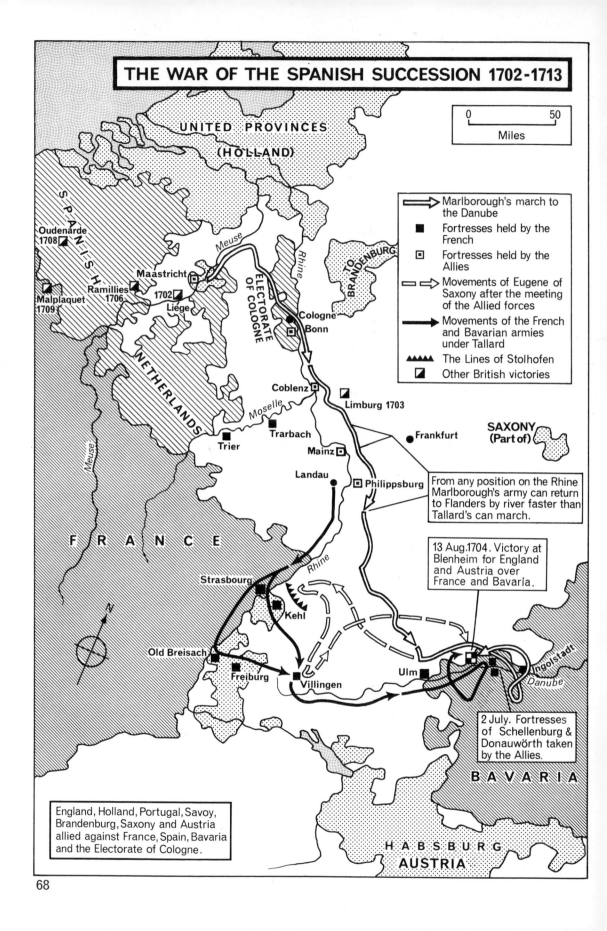

# THE WAR OF THE SPANISH SUCCESSION 1702-1713

UNITED PROVINCES
(HOLLAND)

0       50

Miles

SPANISH

Oudenarde 1708

Maastricht

Ramillies 1706
1702
Liège

Malplaquet 1709

NETHERLANDS

ELECTORATE OF COLOGNE

Cologne
Bonn

TO BRANDENBURG

**Legend:**
- Marlborough's march to the Danube
- ■ Fortresses held by the French
- ◧ Fortresses held by the Allies
- ▭⇢ Movements of Eugene of Saxony after the meeting of the Allied forces
- → Movements of the French and Bavarian armies under Tallard
- ▲▲▲ The Lines of Stolhofen
- ◪ Other British victories

Meuse

Rhine

Coblenz
Limburg 1703

Moselle

Meuse

Trarbach

Trier

Frankfurt

SAXONY (Part of)

Mainz

Landau

Philippsburg

From any position on the Rhine Marlborough's army can return to Flanders by river faster than Tallard's can march.

FRANCE

13 Aug. 1704. Victory at Blenheim for England and Austria over France and Bavaria.

Rhine

Strasbourg

Kehl

Old Breisach

Freiburg

Villingen

Ulm

Ingolstadt

Danube

2 July. Fortresses of Schellenburg & Donauwörth taken by the Allies.

BAVARIA

England, Holland, Portugal, Savoy, Brandenburg, Saxony and Austria allied against France, Spain, Bavaria and the Electorate of Cologne.

HABSBURG AUSTRIA

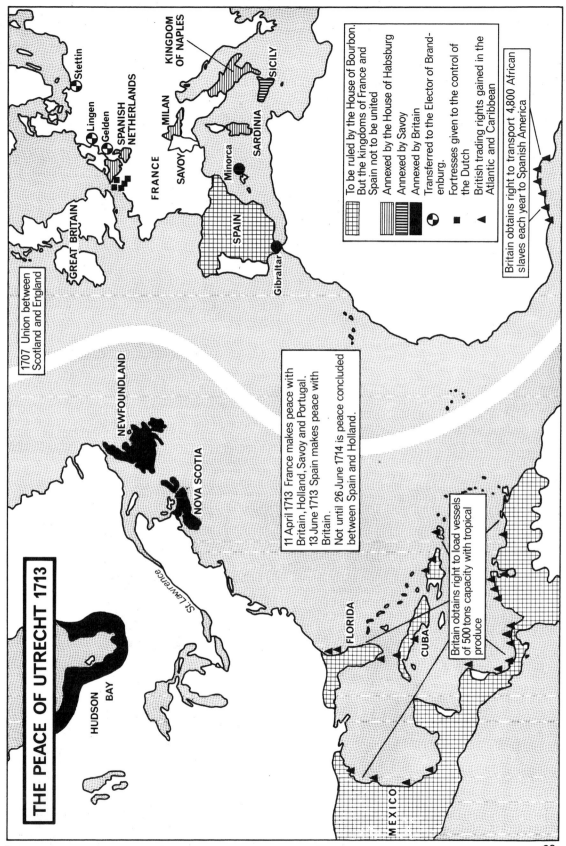

# THE PEACE OF UTRECHT 1713

1707 Union between Scotland and England

**Legend:**
- To be ruled by the House of Bourbon. But the kingdoms of France and Spain not to be united
- Annexed by the House of Habsburg
- Annexed by Savoy
- Annexed by Britain
- Transferred to the Elector of Brandenburg.
- ⊕ Fortresses given to the control of the Dutch
- ▲ British trading rights gained in the Atlantic and Caribbean

Britain obtains right to transport 4,800 African slaves each year to Spanish America

11 April 1713 France makes peace with Britain, Holland, Savoy and Portugal.
13 June 1713 Spain makes peace with Britain.
Not until 26 June 1714 is peace concluded between Spain and Holland.

Britain obtains right to load vessels of 500 tons capacity with tropical produce

HUDSON BAY

St. Lawrence

NEWFOUNDLAND

NOVA SCOTIA

FLORIDA

CUBA

MEXICO

GREAT BRITAIN

Stettin

Lingen
Gelden
SPANISH NETHERLANDS

FRANCE
MILAN
SAVOY
SARDINIA
Minorca
SPAIN
Gibraltar

KINGDOM OF NAPLES
SICILY

E

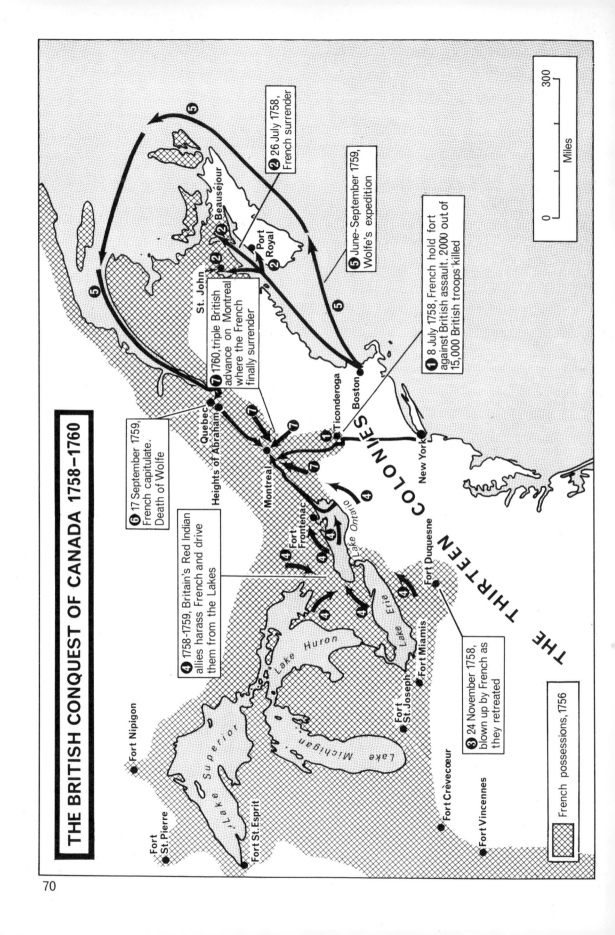

# THE BRITISH CONQUEST OF CANADA 1758–1760

❷ 26 July 1758, French surrender

❺ June–September 1759, Wolfe's expedition

❶ 8 July 1758, French hold fort against British assault. 2000 out of 15,000 British troops killed

❼ 1760, triple British advance on Montreal where the French finally surrender

❻ 17 September 1759, French capitulate. Death of Wolfe

❹ 1758–1759, Britain's Red Indian allies harass French and drive them from the Lakes

❸ 24 November 1758, blown up by French as they retreated

French possessions, 1756

Miles
0                    300

Fort Beauséjour
Port Royal
St. John
Ticonderoga
Boston
New York
Quebec
Heights of Abraham
Montreal
Fort Frontenac
Fort Duquesne
Fort Miamis
Fort St. Joseph
Fort Crèvecoeur
Fort Vincennes
Fort Nipigon
Fort St. Pierre
Fort St. Esprit

Lake Ontario
Lake Erie
Lake Huron
Lake Michigan
Lake Superior

THE THIRTEEN COLONIES

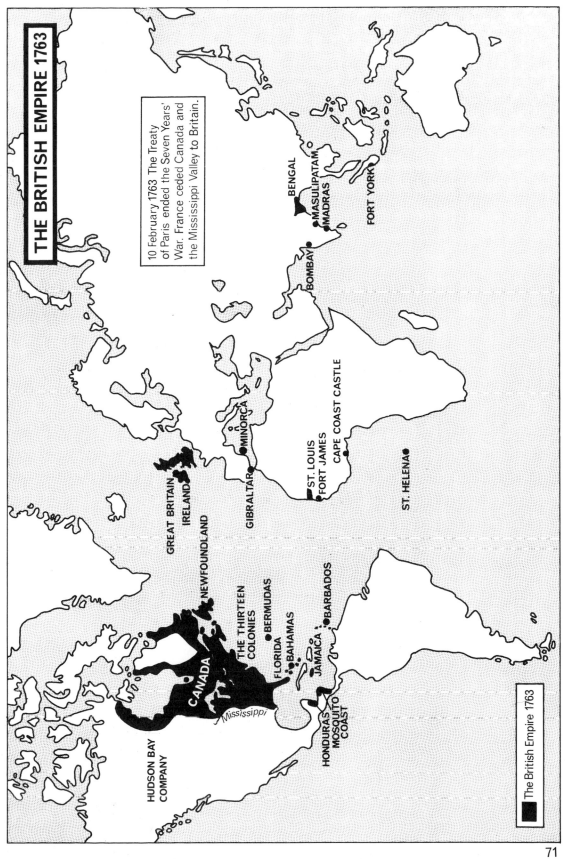

# THE BRITISH EMPIRE 1763

10 February 1763 The Treaty of Paris ended the Seven Years' War. France ceded Canada and the Mississippi Valley to Britain.

BENGAL

MASULIPATAM
MADRAS

FORT YORK

BOMBAY

CAPE COAST CASTLE

MINORCA

ST. LOUIS
FORT JAMES

ST. HELENA

GIBRALTAR

GREAT BRITAIN
IRELAND

NEWFOUNDLAND

THE THIRTEEN
COLONIES
BERMUDAS

FLORIDA
BAHAMAS
JAMAICA
BARBADOS

CANADA

Mississippi

HUDSON BAY
COMPANY

HONDURAS
MOSQUITO
COAST

The British Empire 1763

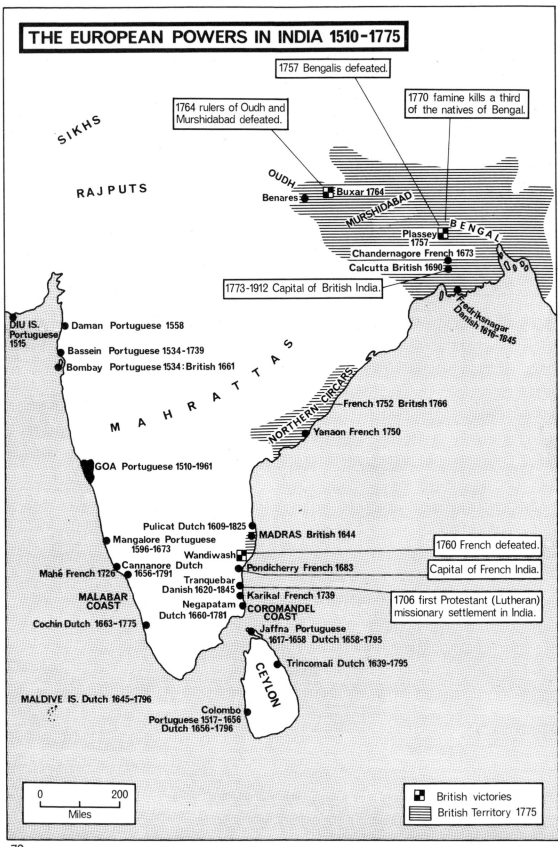

# THE EUROPEAN POWERS IN INDIA 1510-1775

SIKHS

RAJPUTS

1757 Bengalis defeated.

1770 famine kills a third of the natives of Bengal.

1764 rulers of Oudh and Murshidabad defeated.

OUDH

MURSHIDABAD

BENGAL

Benares

Buxar 1764

Plassey 1757

Chandernagore French 1673

Calcutta British 1690

1773-1912 Capital of British India.

Fredriksnagar Danish 1616-1845

DIU IS. Portuguese 1515

Daman Portuguese 1558

Bassein Portuguese 1534-1739

Bombay Portuguese 1534: British 1661

MAHRATTAS

NORTHERN CIRCARS

French 1752 British 1766

Yanaon French 1750

GOA Portuguese 1510-1961

Pulicat Dutch 1609-1825

Mangalore Portuguese 1596-1673

MADRAS British 1644

Wandiwash

1760 French defeated.

Mahé French 1726

Cannanore Dutch 1656-1791

Pondicherry French 1683

Capital of French India.

Tranquebar Danish 1620-1845

Karikal French 1739

1706 first Protestant (Lutheran) missionary settlement in India.

MALABAR COAST

Negapatam Dutch 1660-1781

COROMANDEL COAST

Cochin Dutch 1663-1775

Jaffna Portuguese 1617-1658 Dutch 1658-1795

Trincomali Dutch 1639-1795

CEYLON

MALDIVE IS. Dutch 1645-1796

Colombo Portuguese 1517-1656 Dutch 1656-1796

0 200 Miles

◫ British victories

▤ British Territory 1775

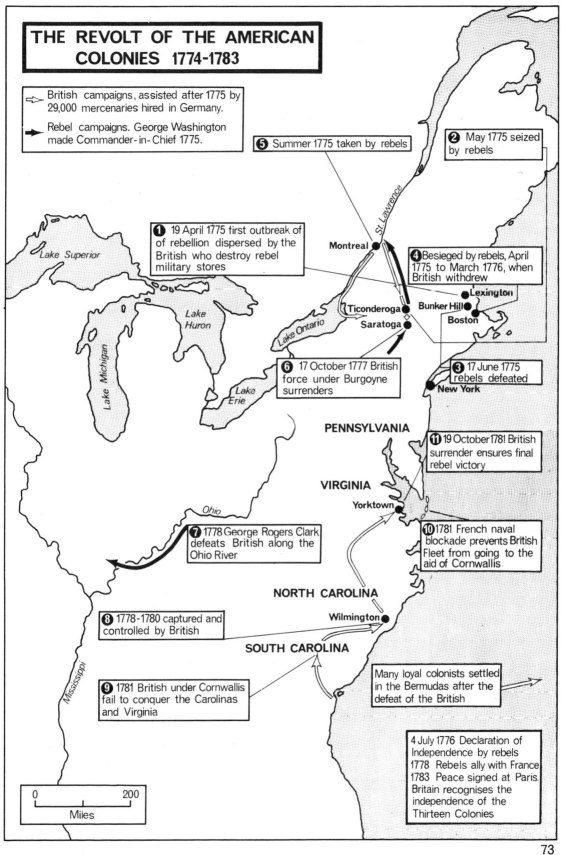

# THE REVOLT OF THE AMERICAN COLONIES 1774-1783

British campaigns, assisted after 1775 by 29,000 mercenaries hired in Germany.

Rebel campaigns. George Washington made Commander-in-Chief 1775.

**⑤** Summer 1775 taken by rebels

**②** May 1775 seized by rebels

**①** 19 April 1775 first outbreak of of rebellion dispersed by the British who destroy rebel military stores

**④** Besieged by rebels, April 1775 to March 1776, when British withdrew

Montreal

Lexington

Ticonderoga

Bunker Hill

Saratoga

Boston

**⑥** 17 October 1777 British force under Burgoyne surrenders

**③** 17 June 1775 rebels defeated

New York

Lake Superior

Lake Huron

Lake Michigan

Lake Ontario

Lake Erie

*St. Lawrence*

**PENNSYLVANIA**

**⑪** 19 October 1781 British surrender ensures final rebel victory

**VIRGINIA**

*Ohio*

Yorktown

**⑩** 1781 French naval blockade prevents British Fleet from going to the aid of Cornwallis

**⑦** 1778 George Rogers Clark defeats British along the Ohio River

**NORTH CAROLINA**

**⑧** 1778-1780 captured and controlled by British

Wilmington

**SOUTH CAROLINA**

*Mississippi*

Many loyal colonists settled in the Bermudas after the defeat of the British

**⑨** 1781 British under Cornwallis fail to conquer the Carolinas and Virginia

4 July 1776 Declaration of Independence by rebels
1778 Rebels ally with France
1783 Peace signed at Paris. Britain recognises the independence of the Thirteen Colonies

0        200
Miles

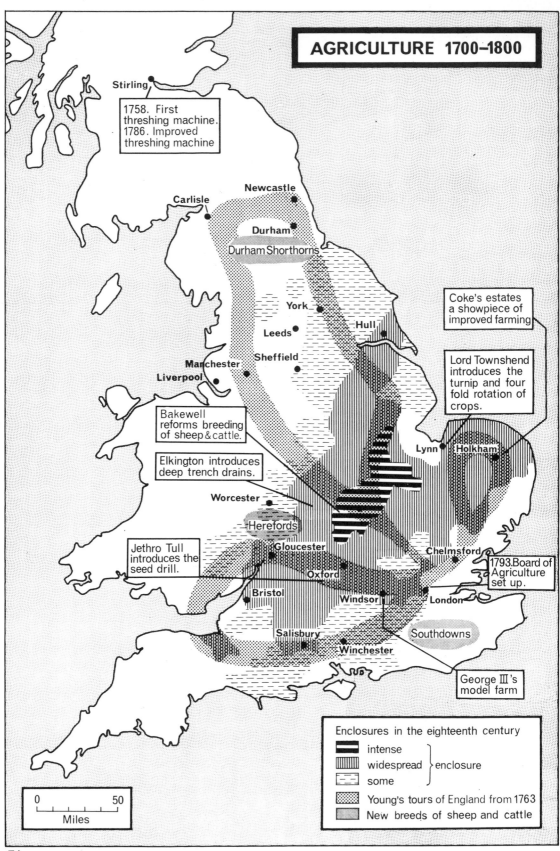

# AGRICULTURE 1700–1800

1758. First threshing machine. 1786. Improved threshing machine

Durham Shorthorns

Coke's estates a showpiece of improved farming

Lord Townshend introduces the turnip and four fold rotation of crops.

Bakewell reforms breeding of sheep & cattle.

Elkington introduces deep trench drains.

Herefords

Jethro Tull introduces the seed drill.

1793. Board of Agriculture set up.

Southdowns

George III's model farm

Stirling

Carlisle

Newcastle

Durham

York

Leeds

Hull

Sheffield

Manchester

Liverpool

Worcester

Gloucester

Lynn

Holkham

Chelmsford

Bristol

Oxford

Windsor

London

Salisbury

Winchester

### Enclosures in the eighteenth century

| | |
|---|---|
| ▬ | intense |
| ▥ | widespread } enclosure |
| ▦ | some |

Young's tours of England from 1763

New breeds of sheep and cattle

0    50
Miles

74

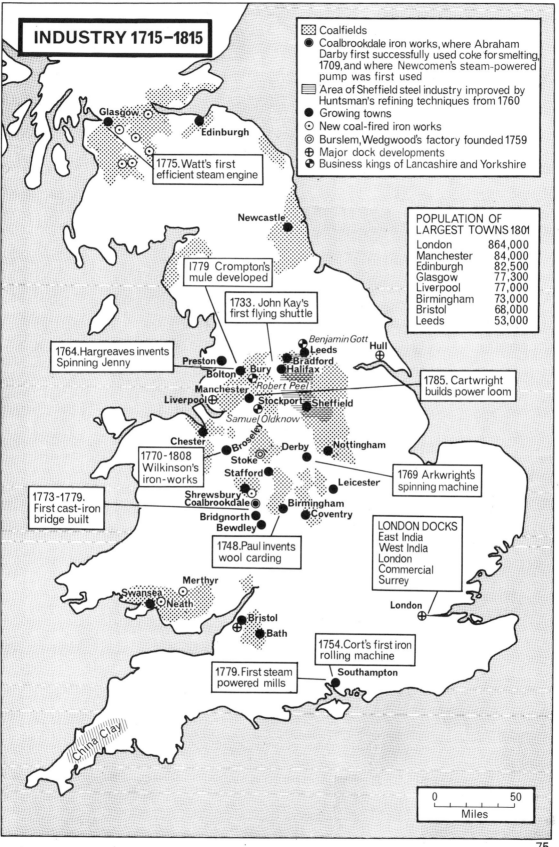

# INDUSTRY 1715–1815

**Legend:**
- Coalfields
- Coalbrookdale iron works, where Abraham Darby first successfully used coke for smelting, 1709, and where Newcomen's steam-powered pump was first used
- Area of Sheffield steel industry improved by Huntsman's refining techniques from 1760
- Growing towns
- New coal-fired iron works
- Burslem, Wedgwood's factory founded 1759
- Major dock developments
- Business kings of Lancashire and Yorkshire

**POPULATION OF LARGEST TOWNS 1801**

| | |
|---|---|
| London | 864,000 |
| Manchester | 84,000 |
| Edinburgh | 82,500 |
| Glasgow | 77,300 |
| Liverpool | 77,000 |
| Birmingham | 73,000 |
| Bristol | 68,000 |
| Leeds | 53,000 |

1775. Watt's first efficient steam engine

1779 Crompton's mule developed

1733. John Kay's first flying shuttle

1764. Hargreaves invents Spinning Jenny

1785. Cartwright builds power loom

1770–1808 Wilkinson's iron-works

1773–1779. First cast-iron bridge built

1748. Paul invents wool carding

1769 Arkwright's spinning machine

LONDON DOCKS
East India
West India
London
Commercial
Surrey

1754. Cort's first iron rolling machine

1779. First steam powered mills

**Place labels:**
Glasgow, Edinburgh, Newcastle, Preston, Bolton, Bury, Manchester, Liverpool, Chester, Stockport, Leeds, Bradford, Halifax, Hull, Sheffield, Broseley, Derby, Nottingham, Stoke, Stafford, Shrewsbury, Coalbrookdale, Bridgnorth, Bewdley, Birmingham, Coventry, Leicester, Merthyr, Swansea, Neath, Bristol, Bath, London, Southampton

*Benjamin Gott*
*Robert Peel*
*Samuel Oldknow*

China Clay

0 — 50 Miles

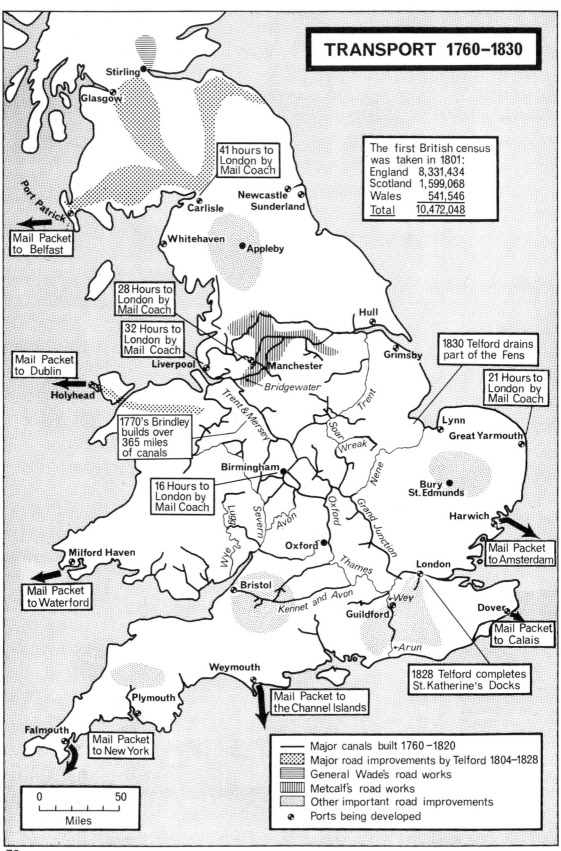

# TRANSPORT 1760–1830

The first British census was taken in 1801:
England 8,331,434
Scotland 1,599,068
Wales 541,546
Total 10,472,048

41 hours to London by Mail Coach

Mail Packet to Belfast

28 Hours to London by Mail Coach

32 Hours to London by Mail Coach

Mail Packet to Dublin

1770's Brindley builds over 365 miles of canals

16 Hours to London by Mail Coach

Mail Packet to Waterford

1830 Telford drains part of the Fens

21 Hours to London by Mail Coach

1828 Telford completes St. Katherine's Docks

Mail Packet to Amsterdam

Mail Packet to Calais

Mail Packet to the Channel Islands

Mail Packet to New York

Stirling
Glasgow
Port Patrick
Carlisle
Newcastle
Sunderland
Whitehaven
Appleby
Hull
Grimsby
Liverpool
Manchester
Bridgewater
Trent & Mersey
Trent
Holyhead
Soar
Wreak
Lynn
Great Yarmouth
Birmingham
Nene
Bury St. Edmunds
Lugg
Severn
Avon
Oxford
Grand Junction
Harwich
Wye
Oxford
Thames
London
Milford Haven
Bristol
Kennet and Avon
Wey
Guildford
Dover
Arun
Weymouth
Plymouth
Falmouth

— Major canals built 1760–1820
Major road improvements by Telford 1804–1828
General Wade's road works
Metcalf's road works
Other important road improvements
Ports being developed

0    50
Miles

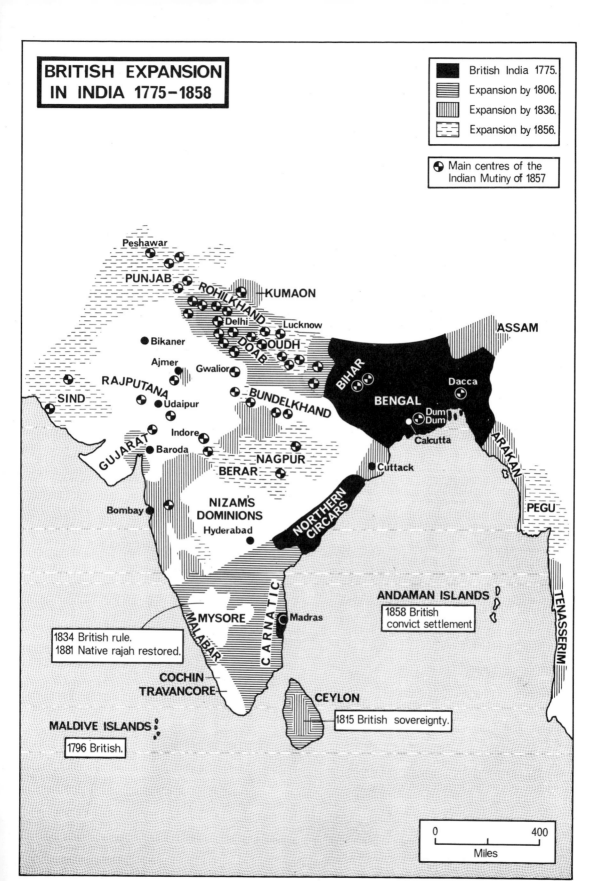

# BRITISH EXPANSION IN INDIA 1775–1858

| | |
|---|---|
| ■ | British India 1775. |
| ☰ | Expansion by 1806. |
| ▥ | Expansion by 1836. |
| ▦ | Expansion by 1856. |

◑ Main centres of the Indian Mutiny of 1857

Peshawar

PUNJAB

ROHILKHAND

KUMAON

Delhi

Lucknow

Bikaner

Ajmer

Gwalior

OUDH

DOAB

RAJPUTANA

SIND

Udaipur

BUNDELKHAND

BIHAR

Dacca

BENGAL

Dum Dum

Calcutta

ARAKAN

Indore

GUJARAT

Baroda

NAGPUR

BERAR

NIZAM'S DOMINIONS

Hyderabad

Cuttack

PEGU

Bombay

NORTHERN CIRCARS

1834 British rule.
1881 Native rajah restored.

MALABAR

MYSORE

CARNATIC

Madras

ANDAMAN ISLANDS

1858 British convict settlement

TENASSERIM

COCHIN
TRAVANCORE

CEYLON

1815 British sovereignty.

MALDIVE ISLANDS

1796 British.

| 0 | | 400 |
|---|---|---|

Miles

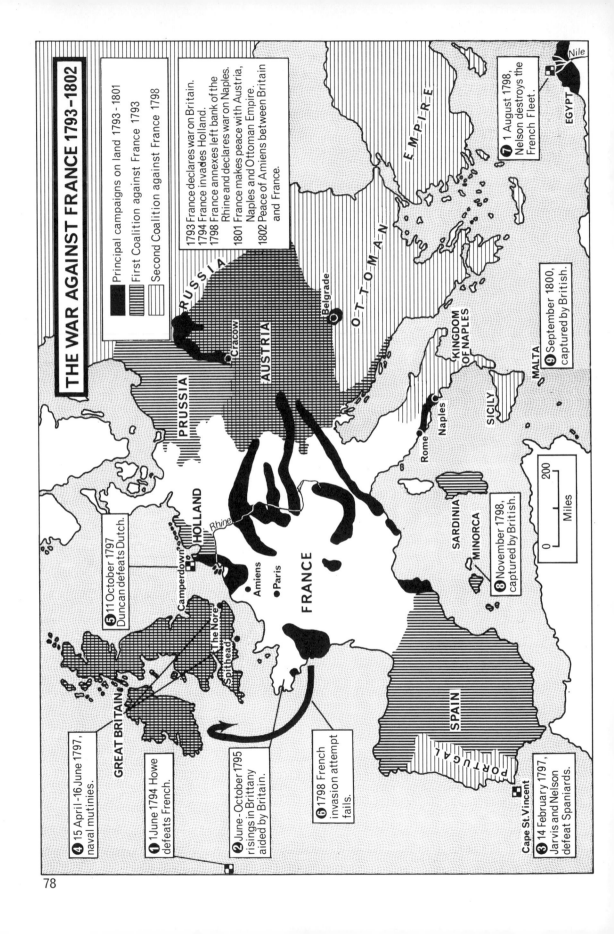

# THE WAR AGAINST FRANCE 1793-1802

Principal campaigns on land 1793 - 1801

First Coalition against France 1793

Second Coalition against France 1798

1793 France declares war on Britain.
1794 France invades Holland.
1798 France annexes left bank of the Rhine and declares war on Naples.
1801 France makes peace with Austria, Naples and Ottoman Empire.
1802 Peace of Amiens between Britain and France.

**EGYPT**

Nile

❼ 1 August 1798, Nelson destroys the French Fleet.

R U S S I A

O T T O M A N   E M P I R E

Belgrade

Cracow

AUSTRIA

PRUSSIA

**MALTA**

❾ September 1800, captured by British.

KINGDOM OF NAPLES

SICILY

Naples

Rome

SARDINIA

HOLLAND

Rhine

❺ 11 October 1797 Duncan defeats Dutch.

Camperdown

The Nore

Spithead

Amiens

Paris

FRANCE

**MINORCA**

❽ November 1798, captured by British.

0    200
Miles

**GREAT BRITAIN**

❹ 15 April-16 June 1797, naval mutinies.

❶ 1 June 1794 Howe defeats French.

❷ June - October 1795 risings in Brittany aided by Britain.

❻ 1798 French invasion attempt fails.

SPAIN

PORTUGAL

Cape St. Vincent

❸ 14 February 1797, Jarvis and Nelson defeat Spaniards.

78

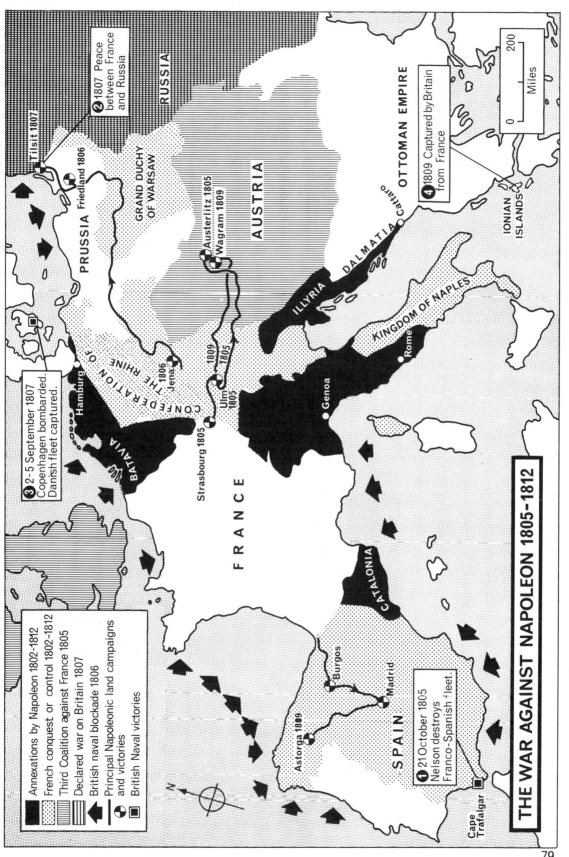

**THE WAR AGAINST NAPOLEON 1805–1812**

RUSSIA

**❷** 1807 Peace between France and Russia

Tilsit 1807

Friedland 1806

PRUSSIA

GRAND DUCHY OF WARSAW

Austerlitz 1805
Wagram 1809

AUSTRIA

OTTOMAN EMPIRE

**❹** 1809 Captured by Britain from France

Cattaro

DALMATIA

ILLYRIA

IONIAN ISLANDS

Jena 1806

CONFEDERATION OF THE RHINE

1809
1805

Ulm 1805

KINGDOM OF NAPLES

Rome

Hamburg

**❸** 2–5 September 1807 Copenhagen bombarded. Danish fleet captured.

BATAVIA

Strasbourg 1805

Genoa

F R A N C E

CATALONIA

Burgos

Madrid

Astorga 1809

S P A I N

**❶** 21 October 1805 Nelson destroys Franco-Spanish fleet.

Cape Trafalgar

200

Miles

0

N

Annexations by Napoleon 1802–1812

French conquest or control 1802–1812

Third Coalition against France 1805

Declared war on Britain 1807

British naval blockade 1806

Principal Napoleonic land campaigns and victories

British Naval victories

79

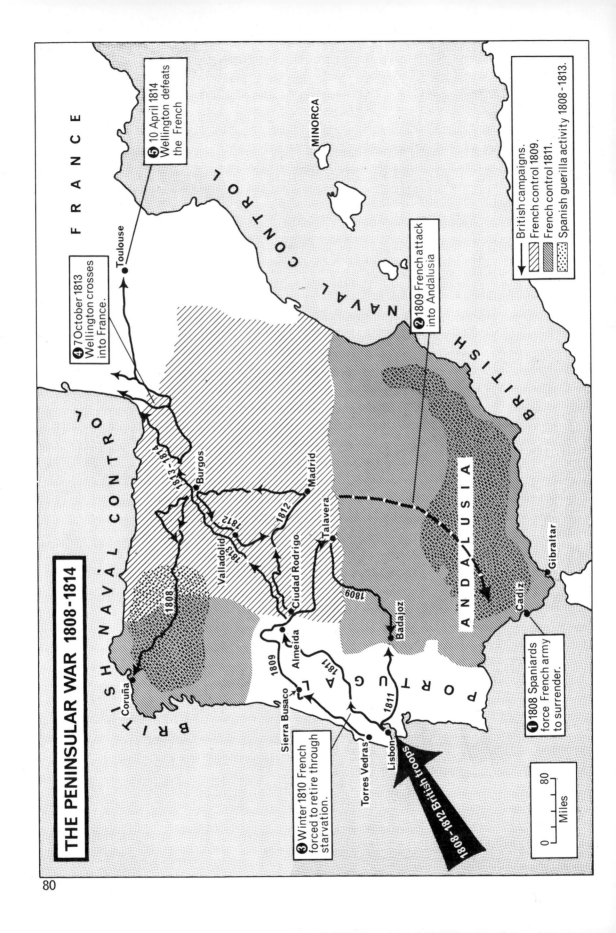

# THE PENINSULAR WAR 1808-1814

**FRANCE**

BRITISH NAVAL CONTROL TO FRANCE

BRITISH NAVAL CONTROL

MINORCA

**4** 7 October 1813 Wellington crosses into France.

**5** 10 April 1814 Wellington defeats the French

**2** 1809 French attack into Andalusia

Toulouse

Coruña

Burgos

1813-1814

1808

Valladolid

1813

1812

Ciudad Rodrigo

1812-

Madrid

Talavera

1809

Badajoz

**A N D A L U S I A**

Cadiz

Gibraltar

Sierra Busaco

Almeida

1809

1811

**P O R T U G A L**

1811

Torres Vedras

Lisbon

1808-1812 British troops

**3** Winter 1810 French forced to retire through starvation.

**1** 1808 Spaniards force French army to surrender.

British campaigns.
French control 1809.
French control 1811.
Spanish guerilla activity 1808-1813.

0        80
Miles

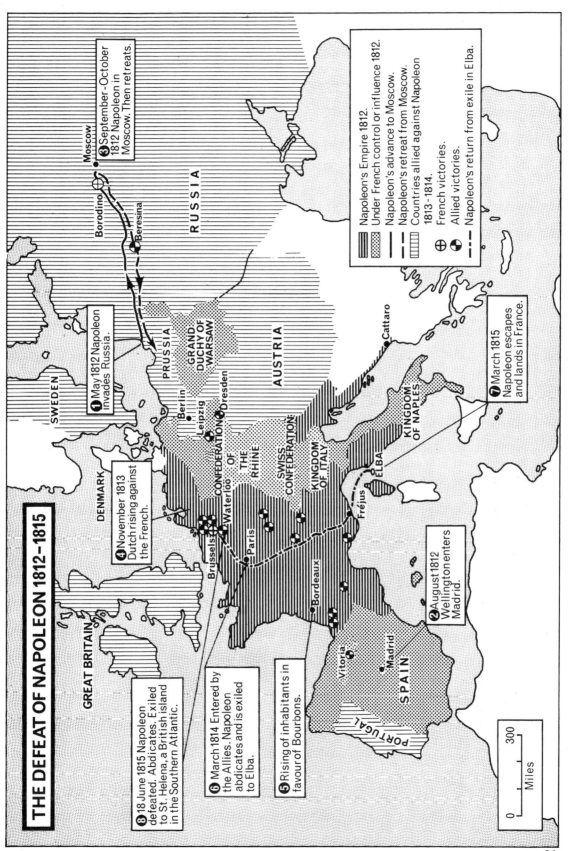

# THE DEFEAT OF NAPOLEON 1812–1815

**1** May 1812 Napoleon invades Russia.

**2** August 1812 Wellington enters Madrid.

**3** September–October 1812 Napoleon in Moscow. Then retreats.

**4** November 1813 Dutch rising against the French.

**5** Rising of inhabitants in favour of Bourbons.

**6** March 1814 Entered by the Allies. Napoleon abdicates and is exiled to Elba.

**7** March 1815 Napoleon escapes and lands in France.

**8** 18 June 1815 Napoleon defeated. Abdicates. Exiled to St. Helena, a British island in the Southern Atlantic.

Napoleon's Empire 1812.

Under French control or influence 1812.

Napoleon's advance to Moscow.

Napoleon's retreat from Moscow.

Countries allied against Napoleon 1813–1814.

French victories.

Allied victories.

Napoleon's return from exile in Elba.

GREAT BRITAIN

SWEDEN

DENMARK

RUSSIA

Moscow

Borodino

Beresina

PRUSSIA

Berlin

GRAND DUCHY OF WARSAW

Leipzig

Dresden

CONFEDERATION OF THE RHINE

Waterloo

Brussels

Paris

AUSTRIA

SWISS CONFEDERATION

KINGDOM OF ITALY

Cattaro

KINGDOM OF NAPLES

ELBA

Fréjus

Bordeaux

Vitoria

Madrid

SPAIN

PORTUGAL

0    300

Miles

81

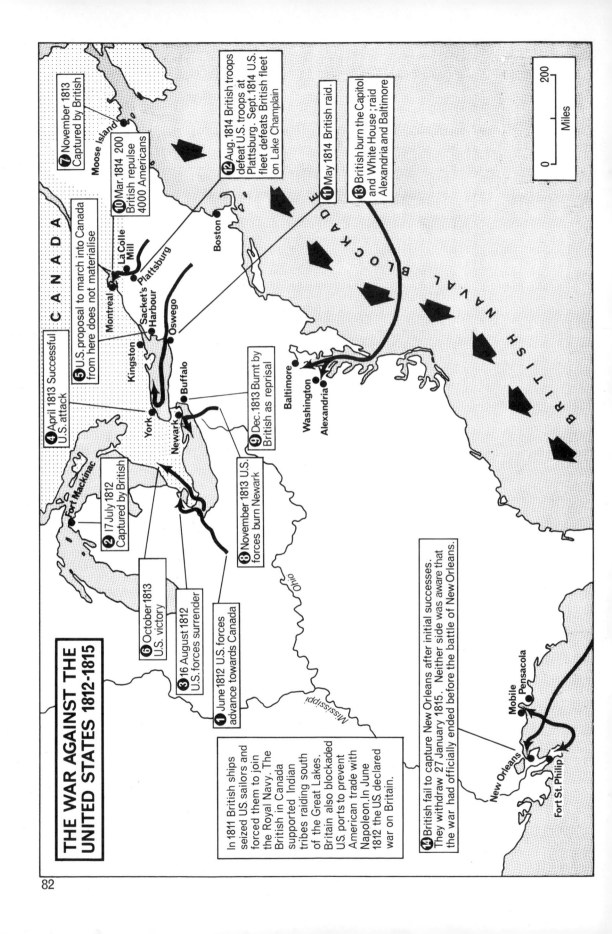

# THE WAR AGAINST THE UNITED STATES 1812-1815

In 1811 British ships seized U.S. sailors and forced them to join the Royal Navy. The British in Canada supported Indian tribes raiding south of the Great Lakes. Britain also blockaded U.S. ports to prevent American trade with Napoleon. In June 1812 the US declared war on Britain.

**1** June 1812 U.S. forces advance towards Canada

**2** 17 July 1812 Captured by British

**3** 16 August 1812 U.S. forces surrender

**4** April 1813 Successful U.S. attack

**5** U.S. proposal to march into Canada from here does not materialise

**6** October 1813 U.S. victory

**7** November 1813 Captured by British

**8** November 1813 U.S. forces burn Newark

**9** Dec. 1813 Burnt by British as reprisal

**10** Mar. 1814 200 British repulse 4000 Americans

**11** May 1814 British raid.

**12** Aug. 1814 British troops defeat U.S. troops at Plattsburg. Sept. 1814 U.S. fleet defeats British fleet on Lake Champlain

**13** British burn the Capitol and White House ; raid Alexandria and Baltimore

**14** British fail to capture New Orleans after initial successes. They withdraw 27 January 1815. Neither side was aware that the war had officially ended before the battle of New Orleans.

BRITISH NAVAL BLOCKADE

CANADA

Moose Island

La Colle Mill

Montreal

Plattsburg

Sacket's Harbour

Kingston

Oswego

Boston

York

Newark

Buffalo

Baltimore

Washington

Alexandria

Fort Mackinac

Ohio

Mississippi

Mobile

Pensacola

New Orleans

Fort St. Philip

200

Miles

0

82

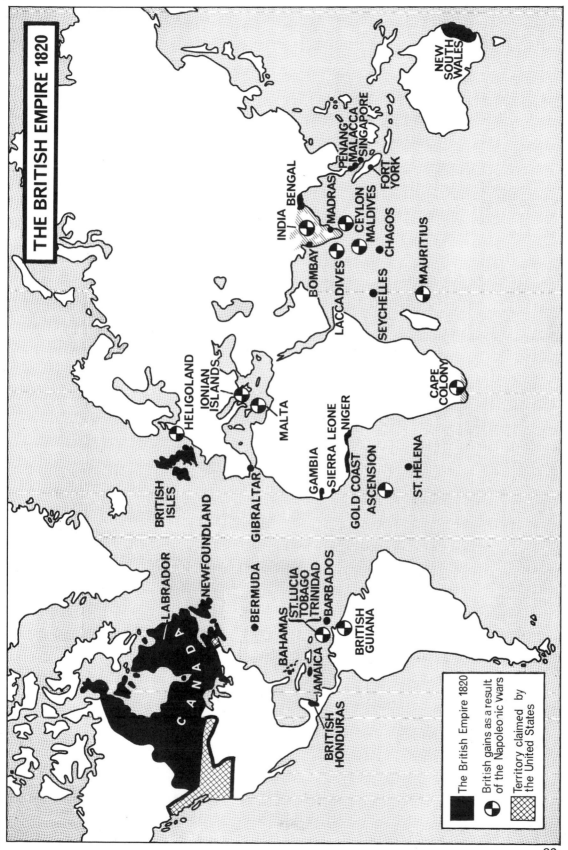

## THE BRITISH EMPIRE 1820

NEW SOUTH WALES

PENANG
MALACCA
SINGAPORE

INDIA
BENGAL
MADRAS
BOMBAY
CEYLON
MALDIVES
LACCADIVES
CHAGOS
FORT YORK

SEYCHELLES
MAURITIUS

HELIGOLAND
IONIAN ISLANDS
MALTA

CAPE COLONY

GAMBIA
SIERRA LEONE
NIGER
GOLD COAST
ASCENSION
ST. HELENA

BRITISH ISLES
GIBRALTAR

LABRADOR
NEWFOUNDLAND

BERMUDA
BAHAMAS
ST. LUCIA
TOBAGO
TRINIDAD
BARBADOS
JAMAICA
BRITISH GUIANA

C A N A D A

BRITISH HONDURAS

The British Empire 1820

British gains as a result of the Napoleonic wars

Territory claimed by the United States

83

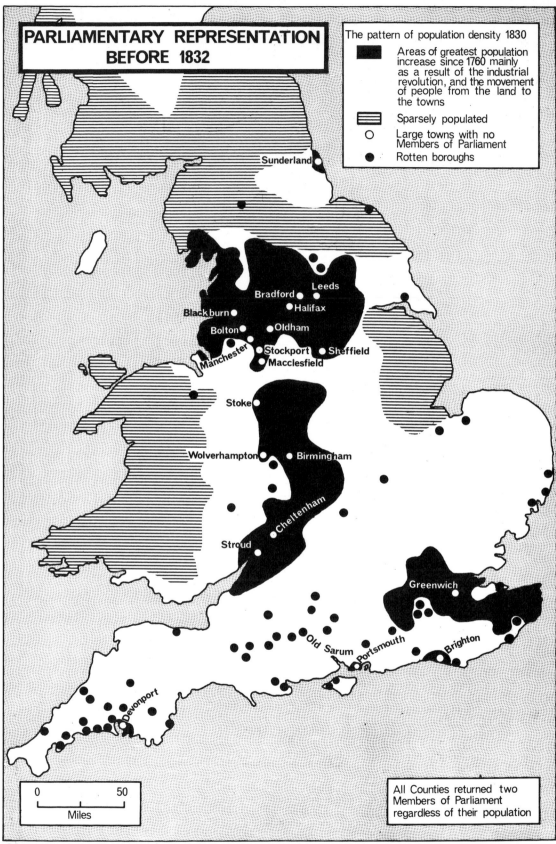

# PARLIAMENTARY REPRESENTATION BEFORE 1832

**The pattern of population density 1830**

- Areas of greatest population increase since 1760 mainly as a result of the industrial revolution, and the movement of people from the land to the towns
- Sparsely populated
- ○ Large towns with no Members of Parliament
- ● Rotten boroughs

Sunderland

Leeds
Bradford
Halifax
Blackburn
Bolton
Oldham
Manchester
Stockport
Sheffield
Macclesfield

Stoke

Wolverhampton
Birmingham

Cheltenham

Stroud

Greenwich

Old Sarum
Portsmouth
Brighton

Devonport

0      50
Miles

All Counties returned two Members of Parliament regardless of their population

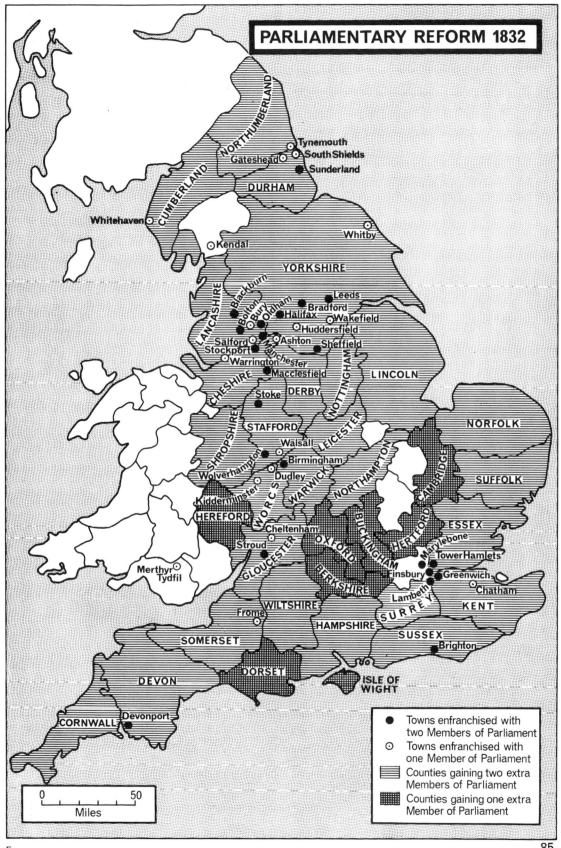

**PARLIAMENTARY REFORM 1832**

NORTHUMBERLAND

Tynemouth
Gateshead
South Shields
Sunderland

DURHAM

Whitehaven

Kendal
Whitby

YORKSHIRE

CUMBERLAND

LANCASHIRE

Blackburn
Bolton
Bury
Oldham
Leeds
Bradford
Halifax
Wakefield
Huddersfield
Salford
Ashton
Stockport
Sheffield
Warrington
Manchester
Macclesfield

CHESHIRE

LINCOLN

Stoke

DERBY

NOTTINGHAM

STAFFORD

LEICESTER

Walsall

NORFOLK

SHROPSHIRE

Wolverhampton
Birmingham
Dudley

WARWICK

NORTHAMPTON

SUFFOLK

Kidderminster

WORCS

HEREFORD

CAMBRIDGE

Cheltenham

HERTFORD

ESSEX

Stroud

OXFORD

BUCKINGHAM

Marylebone
Tower Hamlets

GLOUCESTER

Merthyr Tydfil

BERKSHIRE

Finsbury
Greenwich
Chatham
Lambeth

Frome

WILTSHIRE

SURREY

KENT

HAMPSHIRE

SUSSEX

SOMERSET

Brighton

DORSET

ISLE OF WIGHT

DEVON

Devonport

CORNWALL

- ● Towns enfranchised with two Members of Parliament
- ⊙ Towns enfranchised with one Member of Parliament
- Counties gaining two extra Members of Parliament
- Counties gaining one extra Member of Parliament

0        50
Miles

F

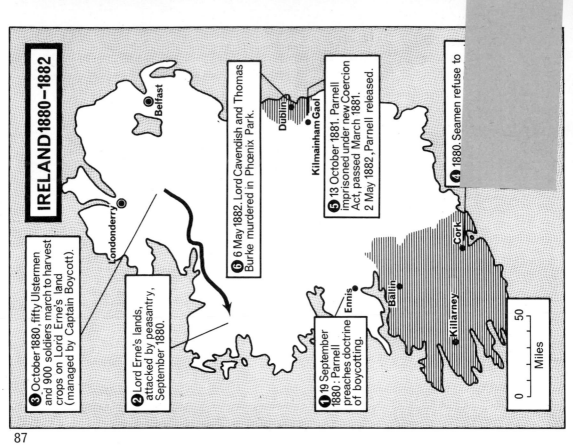

## IRELAND 1880–1882

❸ October 1880, fifty Ulstermen and 900 soldiers march to harvest crops on Lord Erne's land (managed by Captain Boycott).

❷ Lord Erne's lands, attacked by peasantry, September 1880.

❻ 6 May 1882. Lord Cavendish and Thomas Burke murdered in Phœnix Park.

❺ 13 October 1881. Parnell imprisoned under new Coercion Act, passed March 1881. 2 May 1882, Parnell released.

❹ 1880. Seamen refuse to

❶ 19 September 1880 : Parnell preaches doctrine of boycotting.

Belfast

Londonderry

Dublin

Kilmainham Gaol

Ennis

Ballin

Cork

Killarney

0    50
Miles

---

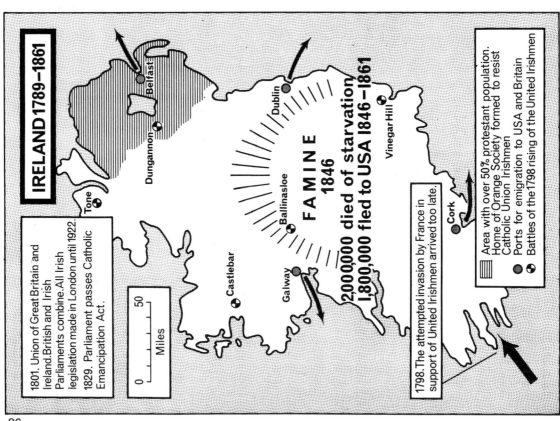

## IRELAND 1789–1861

1801. Union of Great Britain and Ireland. British and Irish Parliaments combine. All Irish legislation made in London until 1922.

1829. Parliament passes Catholic Emancipation Act.

**FAMINE 1846**

**2,000,000 died of starvation 1,800,000 fled to USA 1846–1861**

1798. The attempted invasion by France in support of United Irishmen arrived too late.

Belfast

Dungannon

Tone

Castlebar

Galway

Ballinasloe

Dublin

Vinegar Hill

Cork

Area with over 50% protestant population. Home of Orange Society formed to resist Catholic Union Irishmen

Ports for emigration to USA and Britain

Battles of the 1798 rising of the United Irishmen

0    50
Miles

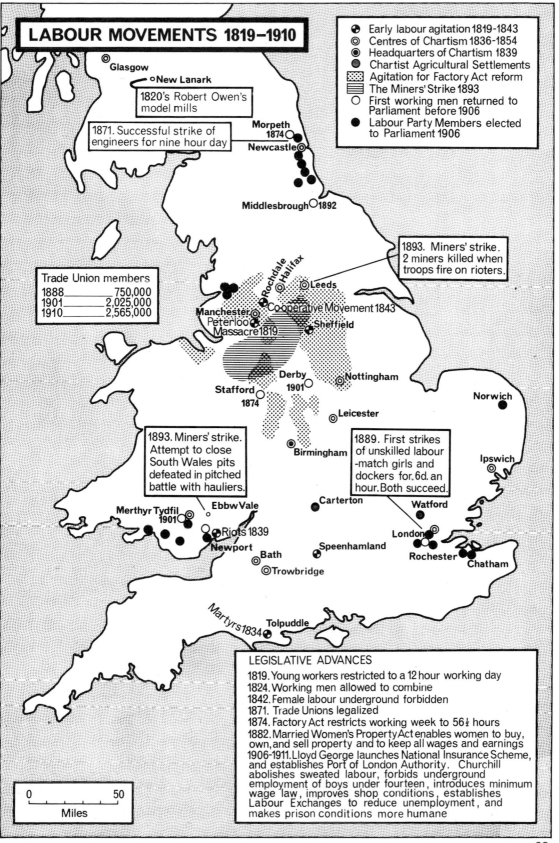

# LABOUR MOVEMENTS 1819–1910

- ◕ Early labour agitation 1819-1843
- ◎ Centres of Chartism 1836-1854
- ◉ Headquarters of Chartism 1839
- ◓ Chartist Agricultural Settlements
- ▦ Agitation for Factory Act reform
- ▤ The Miners' Strike 1893
- ○ First working men returned to Parliament before 1906
- ● Labour Party Members elected to Parliament 1906

**Glasgow**
**New Lanark**
1820's Robert Owen's model mills

1871. Successful strike of engineers for nine hour day

**Morpeth** 1874
**Newcastle**

**Middlesbrough** 1892

1893. Miners' strike. 2 miners killed when troops fire on rioters.

Trade Union members
| 1888 | 750,000 |
| 1901 | 2,025,000 |
| 1910 | 2,565,000 |

**Rochdale** **Halifax**
**Leeds**
**Manchester** Co-operative Movement 1843
**Peterloo** **Sheffield**
Massacre 1819

**Derby** 1901
**Stafford** 1874
**Nottingham**

**Norwich**

**Leicester**

1893. Miners' strike. Attempt to close South Wales pits defeated in pitched battle with hauliers.

**Birmingham**

**Ebbw Vale**

1889. First strikes of unskilled labour -match girls and dockers for 6d. an hour. Both succeed.

**Ipswich**

**Carterton**
**Watford**

**Merthyr Tydfil** 1901
Riots 1839
**Newport**
**Bath**
**Speenhamland**
**London**
**Rochester**
**Chatham**

**Trowbridge**

Martyrs 1834 **Tolpuddle**

## LEGISLATIVE ADVANCES
1819. Young workers restricted to a 12 hour working day
1824. Working men allowed to combine
1842. Female labour underground forbidden
1871. Trade Unions legalized
1874. Factory Act restricts working week to 56½ hours
1882. Married Women's Property Act enables women to buy, own, and sell property and to keep all wages and earnings
1906-1911. Lloyd George launches National Insurance Scheme, and establishes Port of London Authority. Churchill abolishes sweated labour, forbids underground employment of boys under fourteen, introduces minimum wage law, improves shop conditions, establishes Labour Exchanges to reduce unemployment, and makes prison conditions more humane

0    50
Miles

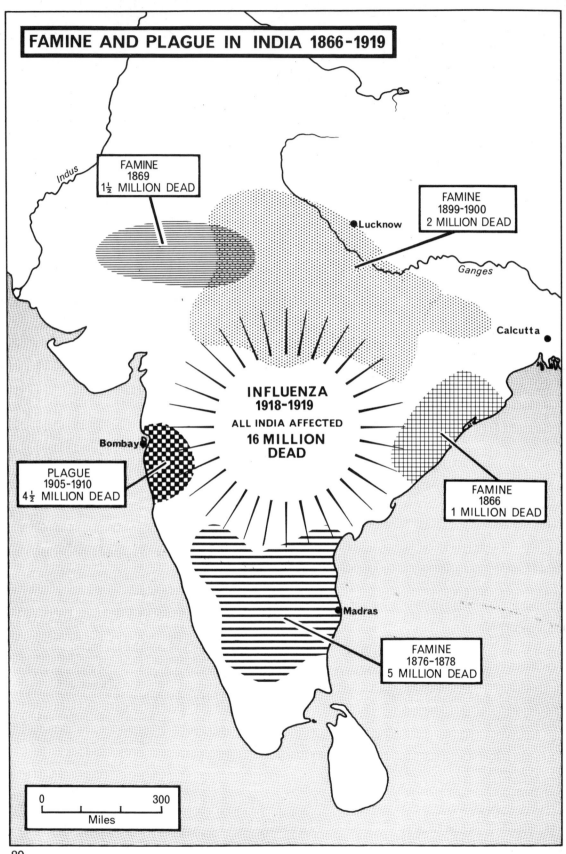

**FAMINE AND PLAGUE IN INDIA 1866-1919**

Indus

FAMINE
1869
1½ MILLION DEAD

Lucknow

FAMINE
1899-1900
2 MILLION DEAD

Ganges

Calcutta

INFLUENZA
1918-1919

ALL INDIA AFFECTED
16 MILLION
DEAD

Bombay

PLAGUE
1905-1910
4½ MILLION DEAD

FAMINE
1866
1 MILLION DEAD

Madras

FAMINE
1876-1878
5 MILLION DEAD

0        300
Miles

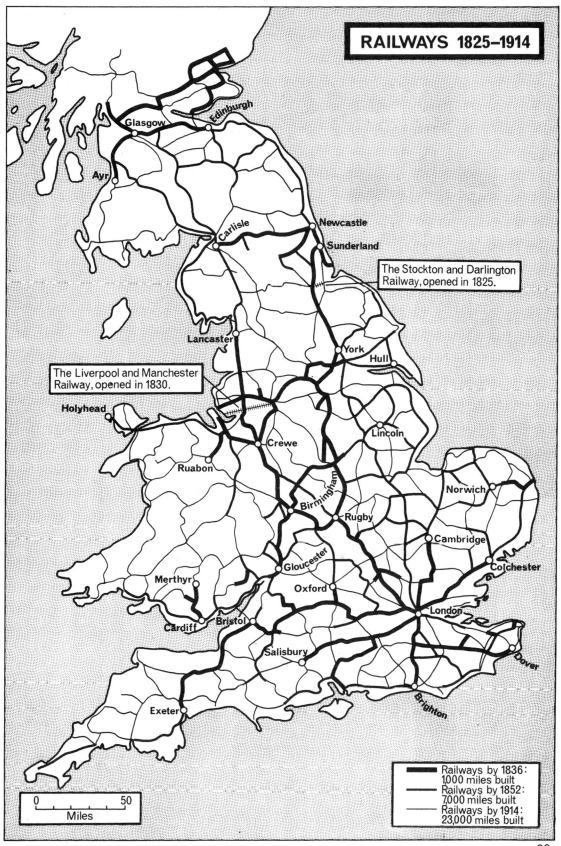

RAILWAYS 1825–1914

The Stockton and Darlington Railway, opened in 1825.

The Liverpool and Manchester Railway, opened in 1830.

Glasgow
Edinburgh
Ayr
Carlisle
Newcastle
Sunderland
Lancaster
York
Hull
Holyhead
Crewe
Lincoln
Ruabon
Norwich
Birmingham
Rugby
Cambridge
Gloucester
Colchester
Merthyr
Oxford
Cardiff
Bristol
London
Salisbury
Dover
Brighton
Exeter

0          50
Miles

Railways by 1836:
1,000 miles built
Railways by 1852:
7,000 miles built
Railways by 1914:
23,000 miles built

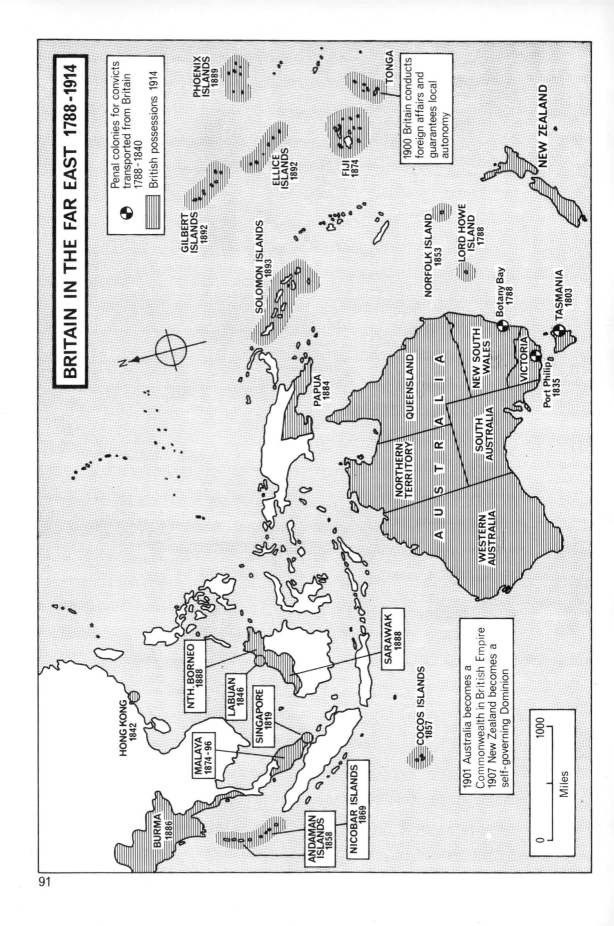

# BRITAIN IN THE FAR EAST 1788-1914

**Penal colonies for convicts transported from Britain 1788-1840**

**British possessions 1914**

1900 Britain conducts foreign affairs and guarantees local autonomy

PHOENIX ISLANDS 1889

TONGA

ELLICE ISLANDS 1892

FIJI 1874

GILBERT ISLANDS 1892

SOLOMON ISLANDS 1893

NEW ZEALAND

NORFOLK ISLAND 1853

LORD HOWE ISLAND 1788

PAPUA 1884

Botany Bay 1788

TASMANIA 1803

N

QUEENSLAND

NEW SOUTH WALES

VICTORIA

Port Philip 1835

NORTHERN TERRITORY

A U S T R A L I A

SOUTH AUSTRALIA

WESTERN AUSTRALIA

HONG KONG 1842

NTH. BORNEO 1888

LABUAN 1846

SINGAPORE 1819

SARAWAK 1888

MALAYA 1874-96

COCOS ISLANDS 1857

1901 Australia becomes a Commonwealth in British Empire
1907 New Zealand becomes a self-governing Dominion

BURMA 1886

ANDAMAN ISLANDS 1858

NICOBAR ISLANDS 1869

0    1000

Miles

91

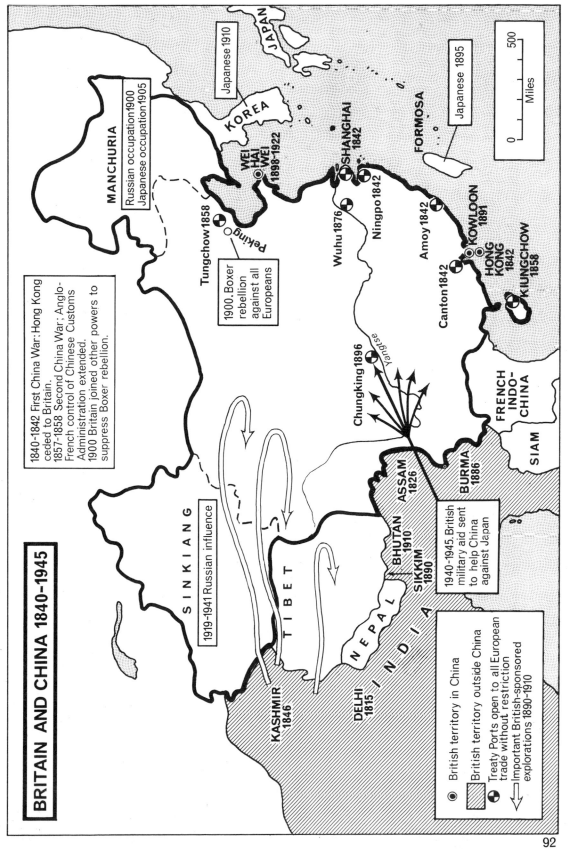

# BRITAIN AND CHINA 1840-1945

MANCHURIA

Russian occupation1900
Japanese occupation1905

Japanese 1910

KOREA

JAPAN

Japanese 1895

FORMOSA

Japanese 1895

0   500
Miles

WEI HAI WEI
1898-1922

SHANGHAI
1842

Tungchow 1858

Peking

1900. Boxer
rebellion
against all
Europeans

Wuhu 1876

Ningpo 1842

Amoy 1842

Canton1842

KOWLOON
1891

HONG
KONG
1842

KIUNGCHOW
1858

Chungking 1896

Yangtse

FRENCH
INDO-
CHINA

SIAM

1840-1842 First China War: Hong Kong
ceded to Britain.
1857-1858 Second China War; Anglo-
French control of Chinese Customs
Administration extended.
1900 Britain joined other powers to
suppress Boxer rebellion.

SINKIANG

1919-1941 Russian influence

TIBET

NEPAL

BHUTAN
1910

ASSAM
1826

BURMA
1886

1940-1945. British
military aid sent
to help China
against Japan

SIKKIM
1890

INDIA

KASHMIR
1846

DELHI
1815

● British territory in China

▨ British territory outside China

◑ Treaty Ports open to all European
trade without restriction

→ Important British-sponsored
explorations 1890-1910

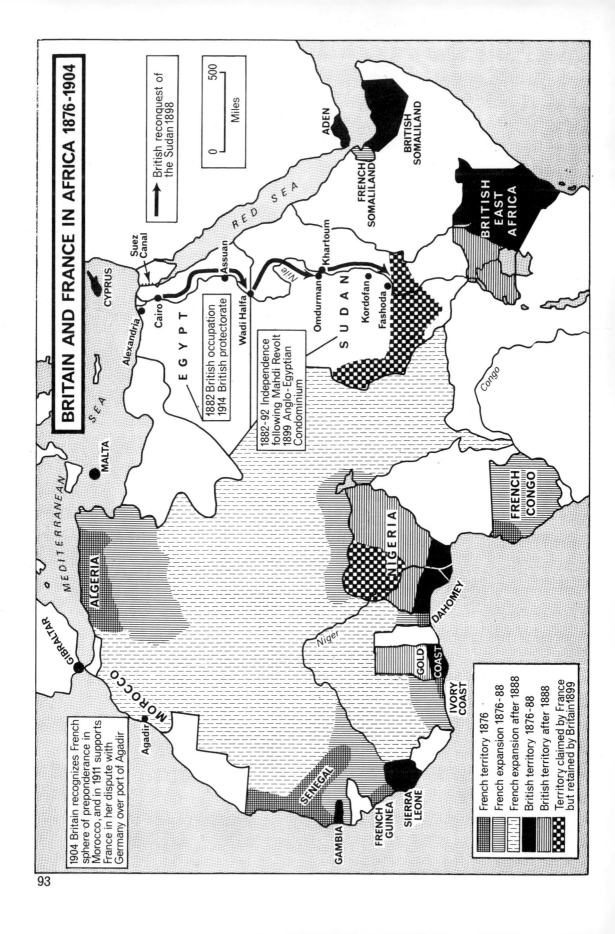

## BRITAIN AND FRANCE IN AFRICA 1876-1904

British reconquest of
the Sudan 1898

500

Miles

0

MEDITERRANEAN SEA

GIBRALTAR

MOROCCO

Agadir

ALGERIA

MALTA

CYPRUS

Alexandria

Cairo

Suez Canal

EGYPT

1882 British occupation
1914 British protectorate

RED SEA

ADEN

FRENCH SOMALILAND

BRITISH SOMALILAND

Assuan

Wadi Halfa

Nile

Khartoum

Omdurman

Kordofan

Fashoda

SUDAN

1882-92 Independence
following Mahdi Revolt
1899 Anglo-Egyptian
Condominium

BRITISH EAST AFRICA

Congo

FRENCH CONGO

NIGERIA

Niger

DAHOMEY

GOLD COAST

IVORY COAST

SENEGAL

FRENCH GUINEA

SIERRA LEONE

GAMBIA

1904 Britain recognizes French
sphere of preponderance in
Morocco, and in 1911 supports
France in her dispute with
Germany over port of Agadir

French territory 1876

French expansion 1876-88

French expansion after 1888

British territory 1876-88

British territory after 1888

Territory claimed by France
but retained by Britain 1899

93

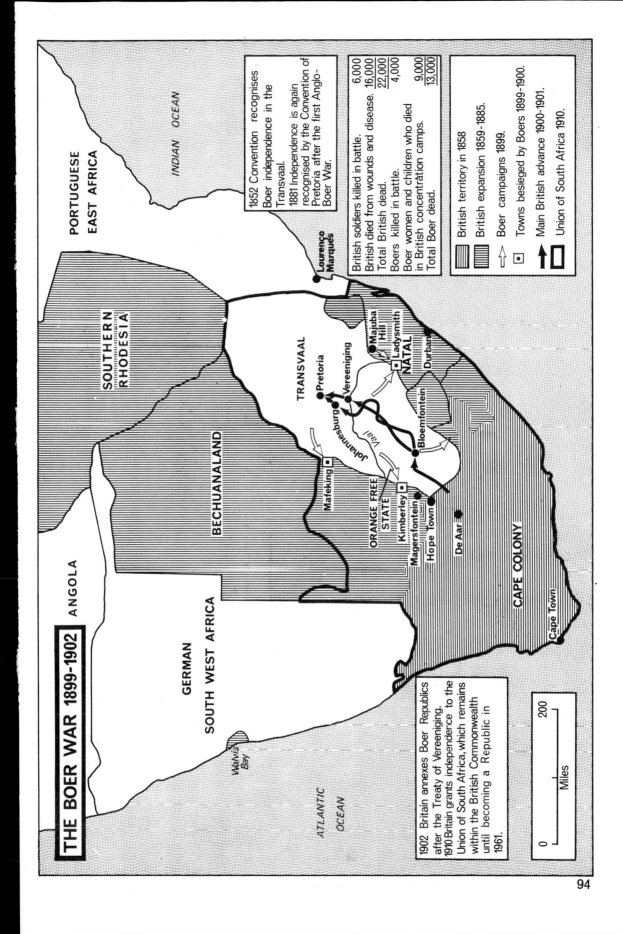

# THE BOER WAR 1899-1902

INDIAN OCEAN

PORTUGUESE EAST AFRICA

ANGOLA

GERMAN SOUTH WEST AFRICA

SOUTHERN RHODESIA

BECHUANALAND

TRANSVAAL

ORANGE FREE STATE

NATAL

CAPE COLONY

ATLANTIC OCEAN

Walvis Bay

Lourenço Marques

Majuba Hill

Ladysmith

Durban

Pretoria

Vereeniging

Johannesburg

Vaal

Bloemfontein

Mafeking

Magersfontein

Kimberley

Hope Town

De Aar

Cape Town

1852 Convention recognises Boer independence in the Transvaal.
1881 Independence is again recognised by the Convention of Pretoria after the first Anglo-Boer War.

| | |
|---|---|
| British soldiers killed in battle. | 6,000 |
| British died from wounds and disease. | 16,000 |
| Total British dead. | 22,000 |
| Boers killed in battle. | 4,000 |
| Boer women and children who died in British concentration camps. | 9,000 |
| Total Boer dead. | 13,000 |

British territory in 1858

British expansion 1859- 1885.

Boer campaigns 1899.

Towns besieged by Boers 1899-1900.

Main British advance 1900-1901.

Union of South Africa 1910.

1902 Britain annexes Boer Republics after the Treaty of Vereeniging.
1910 Britain grants independence to the Union of South Africa, which remains within the British Commonwealth until becoming a Republic in 1961.

0    200

Miles

94

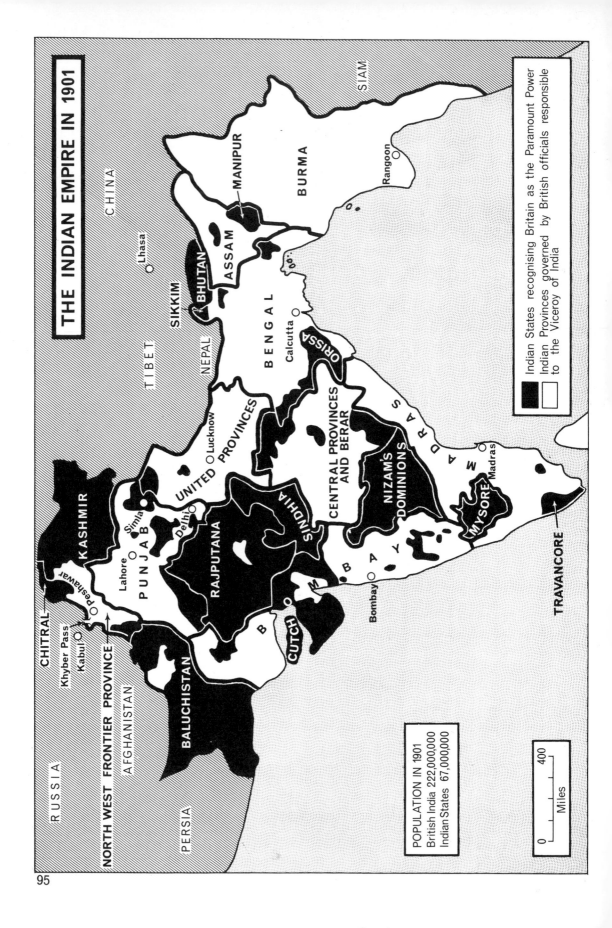

# THE INDIAN EMPIRE IN 1901

RUSSIA

PERSIA

AFGHANISTAN

CHINA

TIBET

SIAM

Lhasa

NORTH WEST FRONTIER PROVINCE

Kabul
Khyber Pass
Peshawar

CHITRAL

KASHMIR

NEPAL

SIKKIM

BHUTAN

BALUCHISTAN

PUNJAB

Lahore
Simla
Delhi

UNITED
PROVINCES

Lucknow

ASSAM

MANIPUR

BENGAL

Calcutta

BURMA

Rangoon

RAJPUTANA

SINDHIA

CUTCH

B

CENTRAL PROVINCES
AND BERAR

ORISSA

M  B  A  Y

Bombay

NIZAM'S
DOMINIONS

M  A  D  R  A  S

MYSORE

Madras

TRAVANCORE

POPULATION IN 1901
British India 222,000,000
Indian States 67,000,000

■ Indian States recognising Britain as the Paramount Power
□ Indian Provinces governed by British officials responsible
   to the Viceroy of India

0        400
Miles

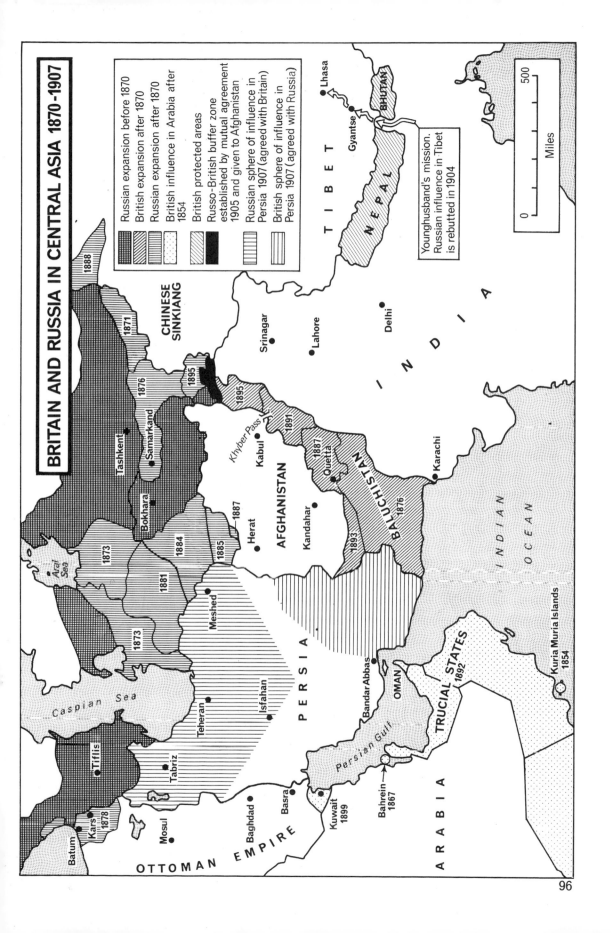

# BRITAIN AND RUSSIA IN CENTRAL ASIA 1870-1907

Russian expansion before 1870

British expansion after 1870

Russian expansion after 1870

British influence in Arabia after 1854

British protected areas

Russo-British buffer zone established by mutual agreement 1905 and given to Afghanistan

Russian sphere of influence in Persia 1907 (agreed with Britain)

British sphere of influence in Persia 1907 (agreed with Russia)

Younghusband's mission. Russian influence in Tibet is rebutted in 1904

500

Miles

0

TIBET

NEPAL

BHUTAN

Lhasa

Gyantse

CHINESE SINKIANG

1888

1871

1876

1895

1895

1891

Srinagar

Lahore

Delhi

INDIA

Tashkent

Samarkand

Khyber Pass

Kabul

1887

Quetta

Karachi

Bokhara

1887

AFGHANISTAN

Herat

Kandahar

BALUCHISTAN

1876

1893

Aral Sea

1873

1884

1885

1881

Meshed

INDIAN OCEAN

1873

Isfahan

PERSIA

Caspian Sea

Teheran

Bandar Abbas

OMAN

Kuria Muria Islands 1854

Tiflis

Tabriz

Persian Gulf

TRUCIAL STATES 1892

Kars 1878

Batum

Basra

Bahrein 1867

Kuwait 1899

ARABIA

Mosul

Baghdad

OTTOMAN EMPIRE

96

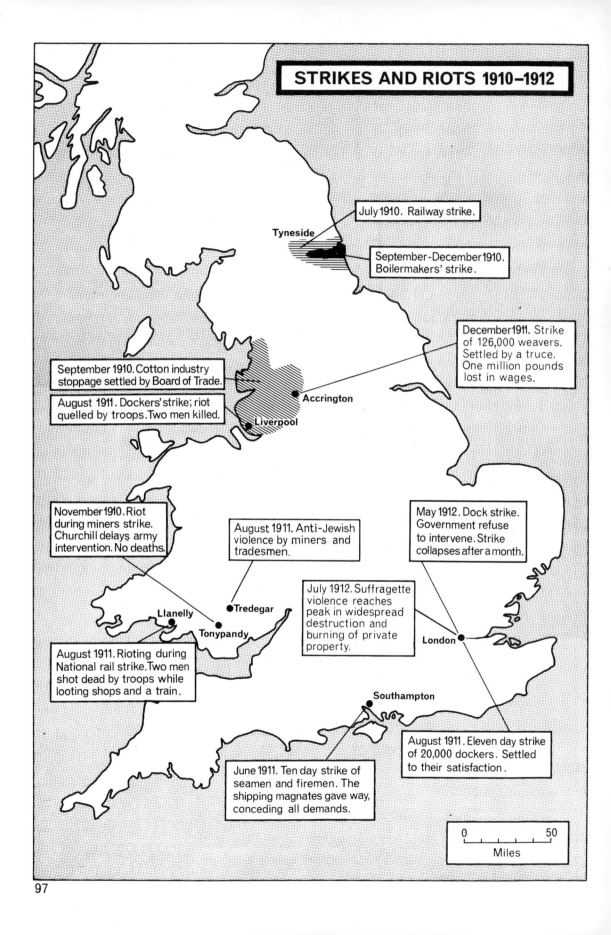

# STRIKES AND RIOTS 1910–1912

July 1910. Railway strike.

Tyneside

September–December 1910. Boilermakers' strike.

December 1911. Strike of 126,000 weavers. Settled by a truce. One million pounds lost in wages.

September 1910. Cotton industry stoppage settled by Board of Trade.

August 1911. Dockers' strike; riot quelled by troops. Two men killed.

Accrington

Liverpool

November 1910. Riot during miners strike. Churchill delays army intervention. No deaths.

August 1911. Anti-Jewish violence by miners and tradesmen.

May 1912. Dock strike. Government refuse to intervene. Strike collapses after a month.

July 1912. Suffragette violence reaches peak in widespread destruction and burning of private property.

Tredegar

Llanelly

Tonypandy

London

August 1911. Rioting during National rail strike. Two men shot dead by troops while looting shops and a train.

Southampton

August 1911. Eleven day strike of 20,000 dockers. Settled to their satisfaction.

June 1911. Ten day strike of seamen and firemen. The shipping magnates gave way, conceding all demands.

0     50
Miles

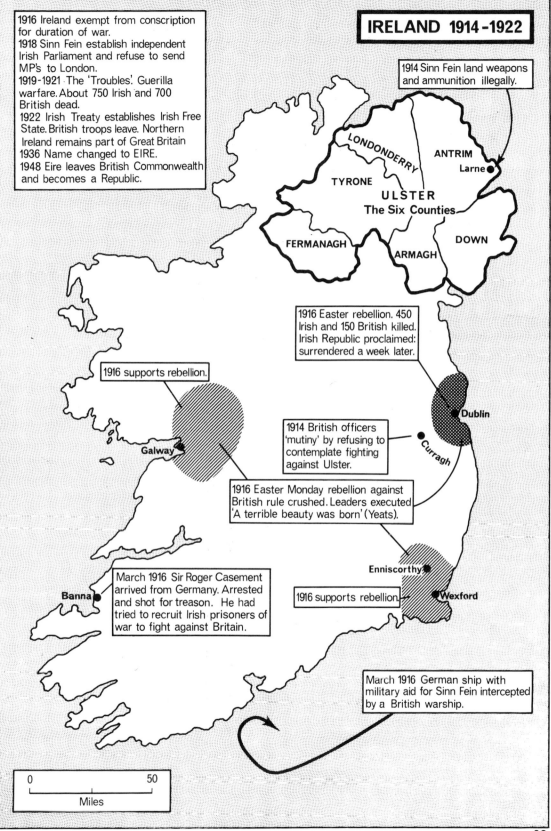

# IRELAND 1914-1922

1916 Ireland exempt from conscription for duration of war.
1918 Sinn Fein establish independent Irish Parliament and refuse to send MP's to London.
1919-1921 The 'Troubles'. Guerilla warfare. About 750 Irish and 700 British dead.
1922 Irish Treaty establishes Irish Free State. British troops leave. Northern Ireland remains part of Great Britain
1936 Name changed to EIRE.
1948 Eire leaves British Commonwealth and becomes a Republic.

1914 Sinn Fein land weapons and ammunition illegally.

LONDONDERRY
ANTRIM
Larne
TYRONE
ULSTER
The Six Counties
FERMANAGH
DOWN
ARMAGH

1916 Easter rebellion. 450 Irish and 150 British killed. Irish Republic proclaimed: surrendered a week later.

1916 supports rebellion.

Galway

Dublin

1914 British officers 'mutiny' by refusing to contemplate fighting against Ulster.

Curragh

1916 Easter Monday rebellion against British rule crushed. Leaders executed 'A terrible beauty was born' (Yeats).

Enniscorthy

March 1916 Sir Roger Casement arrived from Germany. Arrested and shot for treason. He had tried to recruit Irish prisoners of war to fight against Britain.

Banna

1916 supports rebellion.

Wexford

March 1916 German ship with military aid for Sinn Fein intercepted by a British warship.

0        50
Miles

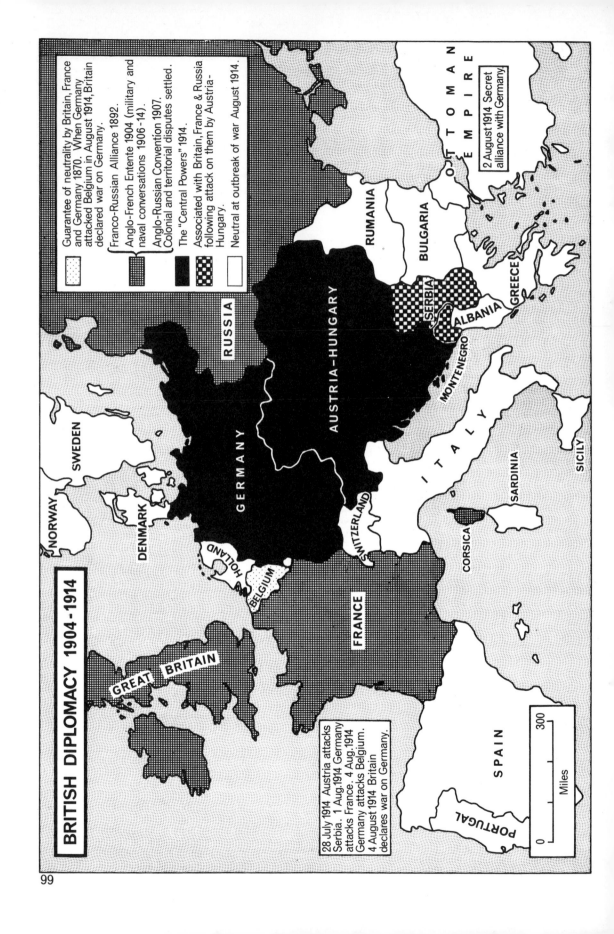

BRITISH DIPLOMACY 1904-1914

Guarantee of neutrality by Britain, France and Germany 1870. When Germany attacked Belgium in August 1914, Britain declared war on Germany.

Franco-Russian Alliance 1892.

Anglo-French Entente 1904 (military and naval conversations 1906-14).

Anglo-Russian Convention 1907. Colonial and territorial disputes settled.

The "Central Powers" 1914.

Associated with Britain, France & Russia following attack on them by Austria-Hungary.

Neutral at outbreak of war August 1914.

2 August 1914 Secret alliance with Germany.

28 July 1914 Austria attacks Serbia. 1 Aug.1914 Germany attacks France. 4 Aug.1914 Germany attacks Belgium. 4 August 1914 Britain declares war on Germany.

NORWAY

SWEDEN

DENMARK

GREAT BRITAIN

HOLLAND

BELGIUM

GERMANY

RUSSIA

FRANCE

SWITZERLAND

AUSTRIA-HUNGARY

RUMANIA

SERBIA

MONTENEGRO

ALBANIA

BULGARIA

GREECE

ITALY

CORSICA

SARDINIA

SICILY

SPAIN

PORTUGAL

OTTOMAN EMPIRE

0    300
Miles

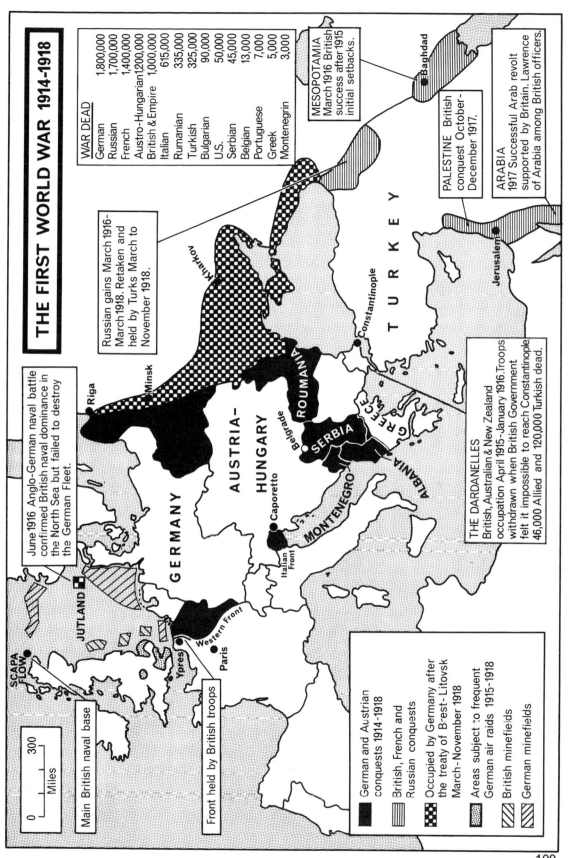

# THE FIRST WORLD WAR 1914-1918

| WAR DEAD | |
|---|---|
| German | 1,800,000 |
| Russian | 1,700,000 |
| French | 1,400,000 |
| Austro-Hungarian | 1,200,000 |
| British & Empire | 1,000,000 |
| Italian | 615,000 |
| Rumanian | 335,000 |
| Turkish | 325,000 |
| Bulgarian | 90,000 |
| U.S. | 50,000 |
| Serbian | 45,000 |
| Belgian | 13,000 |
| Portuguese | 7,000 |
| Greek | 5,000 |
| Montenegrin | 3,000 |

MESOPOTAMIA March 1916 British success after 1915 initial setbacks.

PALESTINE British conquest October-December 1917.

ARABIA 1917 Successful Arab revolt supported by Britain. Lawrence of Arabia among British officers.

Russian gains March 1916-March 1918. Retaken and held by Turks March to November 1918.

June 1916 Anglo-German naval battle confirmed British naval dominance in the North Sea but failed to destroy the German Fleet.

THE DARDANELLES British, Australian & New Zealand occupation April 1915-January 1916.Troops withdrawn when British Government felt it impossible to reach Constantinople. 46,000 Allied and 120,000 Turkish dead.

Main British naval base

Front held by British troops

Baghdad

Jerusalem

Constantinople

TURKEY

GREECE

ALBANIA

MONTENEGRO

SERBIA

Belgrade

ROUMANIA

AUSTRIA-HUNGARY

GERMANY

Kharkov

Minsk

Riga

Caporetto

Italian Front

Western Front

Ypres

Paris

JUTLAND

SCAPA FLOW

| | German and Austrian conquests 1914-1918 |
|---|---|
| | British, French and Russian conquests |
| | Occupied by Germany after the treaty of Brest-Litovsk March-November 1918 |
| | Areas subject to frequent German air raids 1915-1918 |
| | British minefields |
| | German minefields |

Miles
0        300

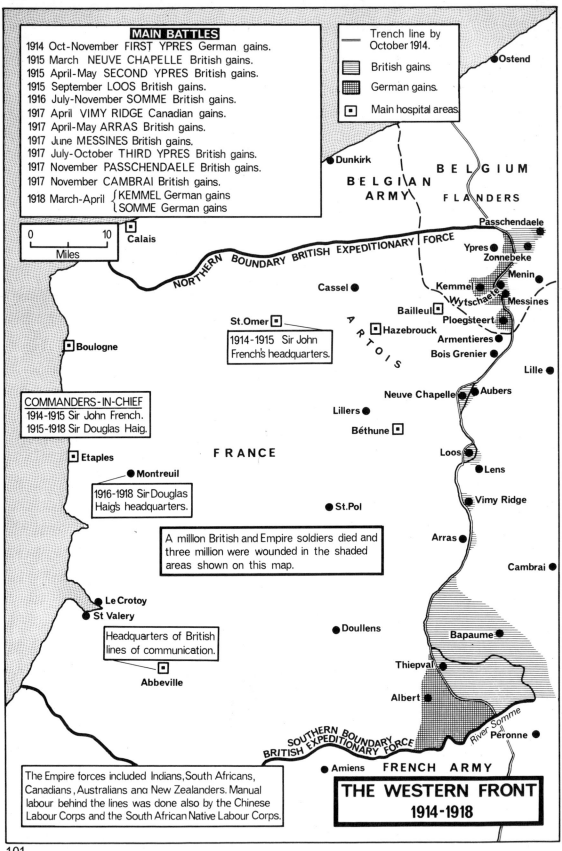

**MAIN BATTLES**

1914 Oct-November FIRST YPRES German gains.
1915 March NEUVE CHAPELLE British gains.
1915 April-May SECOND YPRES British gains.
1915 September LOOS British gains.
1916 July-November SOMME British gains.
1917 April VIMY RIDGE Canadian gains.
1917 April-May ARRAS British gains.
1917 June MESSINES British gains.
1917 July-October THIRD YPRES British gains.
1917 November PASSCHENDAELE British gains.
1917 November CAMBRAI British gains.
1918 March-April { KEMMEL German gains
                  { SOMME German gains

Trench line by October 1914.
British gains.
German gains.
Main hospital areas.

0       10
Miles

Calais

NORTHERN BOUNDARY BRITISH EXPEDITIONARY FORCE

Ostend

BELGIUM

BELGIAN ARMY

FLANDERS

Dunkirk

Passchendaele
Ypres
Zonnebeke
Menin
Kemmel
Wytschaete
Messines
Ploegsteert
Armentieres
Bois Grenier
Lille

St.Omer
1914-1915 Sir John French's headquarters.

Cassel

A R T O I S

Hazebrouck
Bailleul

Boulogne

Neuve Chapelle
Aubers

COMMANDERS-IN-CHIEF
1914-1915 Sir John French.
1915-1918 Sir Douglas Haig.

Lillers
Béthune

F R A N C E

Etaples

Montreuil

1916-1918 Sir Douglas Haig's headquarters.

St.Pol

A million British and Empire soldiers died and three million were wounded in the shaded areas shown on this map.

Loos
Lens
Vimy Ridge
Arras
Cambrai

Le Crotoy
St Valery

Doullens

Bapaume

Headquarters of British lines of communication.

Abbeville

Thiepval

Albert

River Somme
Péronne

SOUTHERN BOUNDARY BRITISH EXPEDITIONARY FORCE

The Empire forces included Indians, South Africans, Canadians, Australians and New Zealanders. Manual labour behind the lines was done also by the Chinese Labour Corps and the South African Native Labour Corps.

Amiens

FRENCH ARMY

**THE WESTERN FRONT 1914-1918**

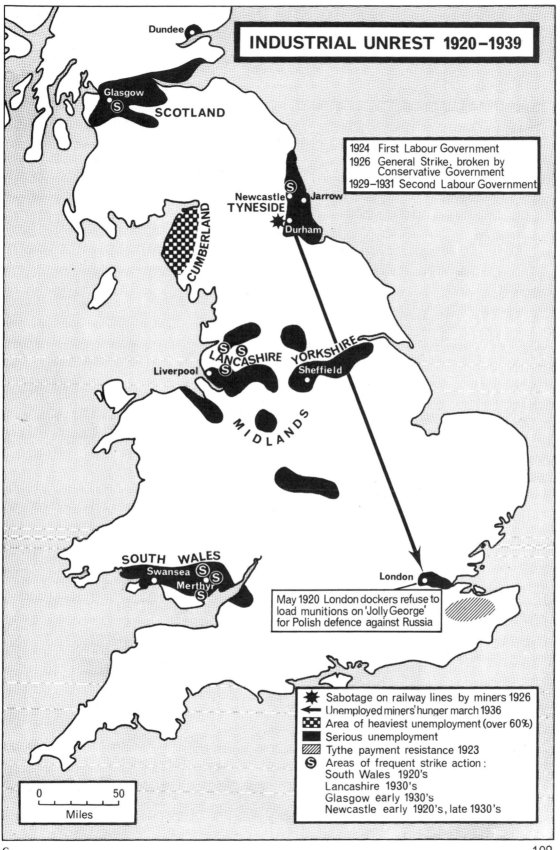

# INDUSTRIAL UNREST 1920–1939

Dundee

Glasgow
(S)

SCOTLAND

1924 First Labour Government
1926 General Strike, broken by
Conservative Government
1929–1931 Second Labour Government

CUMBERLAND

Newcastle
TYNESIDE
(S)
Jarrow
Durham

LANCASHIRE    YORKSHIRE
(S)(S)
(S)    Sheffield
Liverpool

M I D L A N D S

SOUTH WALES
Swansea    (S)(S)
Merthyr
(S)

London

May 1920 London dockers refuse to
load munitions on 'Jolly George'
for Polish defence against Russia

★ Sabotage on railway lines by miners 1926
← Unemployed miners' hunger march 1936
▓ Area of heaviest unemployment (over 60%)
■ Serious unemployment
▨ Tythe payment resistance 1923
(S) Areas of frequent strike action:
South Wales 1920's
Lancashire 1930's
Glasgow early 1930's
Newcastle early 1920's, late 1930's

0    50
Miles

G

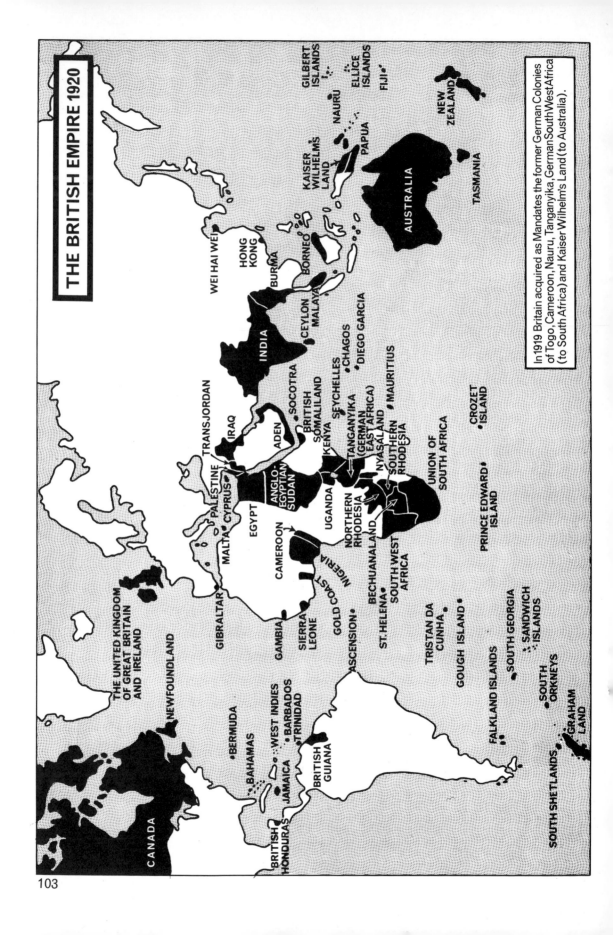

# THE BRITISH EMPIRE 1920

In 1919 Britain acquired as Mandates the former German Colonies of Togo, Cameroon, Nauru, Tanganyika, German South West Africa (to South Africa) and Kaiser Wilhelm's Land (to Australia).

GILBERT ISLANDS

ELLICE ISLANDS

FIJI

NAURU

NEW ZEALAND

TASMANIA

PAPUA

KAISER WILHELM'S LAND

AUSTRALIA

WEI HAI WEI

HONG KONG

BORNEO

BURMA

CEYLON

MALAYA

INDIA

SOCOTRA

BRITISH SOMALILAND

SEYCHELLES

CHAGOS

DIEGO GARCIA

TRANSJORDAN

IRAQ

ADEN

KENYA

TANGANYIKA (GERMAN EAST AFRICA)

NYASALAND

MAURITIUS

SOUTHERN RHODESIA

PALESTINE

MALTA

CYPRUS

PRINCE EDWARD ISLAND

CROZET ISLAND

ANGLO-EGYPTIAN SUDAN

EGYPT

UGANDA

NORTHERN RHODESIA

BECHUANALAND

UNION OF SOUTH AFRICA

CAMEROON

NIGERIA

GOLD COAST

SOUTH WEST AFRICA

GIBRALTAR

GAMBIA

SIERRA LEONE

ASCENSION

ST. HELENA

TRISTAN DA CUNHA

GOUGH ISLAND

SOUTH GEORGIA

SANDWICH ISLANDS

THE UNITED KINGDOM OF GREAT BRITAIN AND IRELAND

NEWFOUNDLAND

BERMUDA

BAHAMAS

JAMAICA

WEST INDIES

BARBADOS

TRINIDAD

BRITISH GUIANA

BRITISH HONDURAS

FALKLAND ISLANDS

SOUTH ORKNEYS

SOUTH SHETLANDS

GRAHAM LAND

CANADA

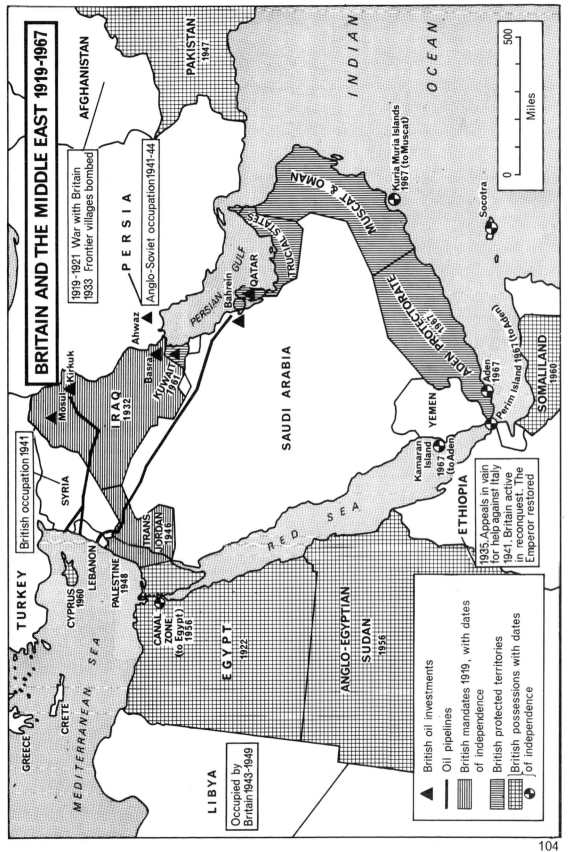

# BRITAIN AND THE MIDDLE EAST 1919-1967

1919-1921  War with Britain
1933  Frontier villages bombed

AFGHANISTAN

PAKISTAN
1947

PERSIA

Anglo-Soviet occupation 1941-44

Ahwaz

TRUCIAL STATES

Bahrein

PERSIAN GULF

QATAR

MUSCAT & OMAN

Kuria Muria Islands
1967 (to Muscat)

Socotra

INDIAN OCEAN

500
Miles
0

Kirkuk

Mosul

IRAQ
1932

Basra

KUWAIT
1961

SAUDI ARABIA

ADEN PROTECTORATE
1967

Aden
1967

Perim Island 1961 (to Aden)

SOMALILAND
1960

British occupation 1941

SYRIA

YEMEN

Kamaran
Island
1967
(to Aden)

ETHIOPIA

1935. Appeals in vain
for help against Italy
1941. Britain active
in reconquest. The
Emperor restored

TURKEY

British occupation 1941

CYPRUS
1960

LEBANON

PALESTINE
1948

TRANS-
JORDAN
1946

RED SEA

CRETE

CANAL
ZONE
(to Egypt)
1956

EGYPT
1922

ANGLO-EGYPTIAN
SUDAN
1956

GREECE

MEDITERRANEAN SEA

LIBYA

Occupied by
Britain 1943-1949

▲  British oil investments
|   Oil pipelines
    British mandates 1919, with dates
    of independence
    British protected territories
    British possessions with dates
    of independence

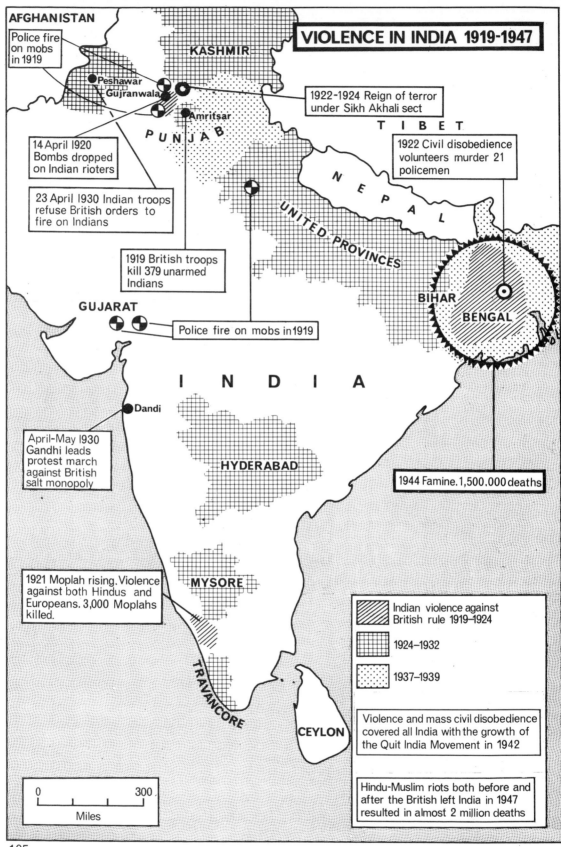

# VIOLENCE IN INDIA 1919-1947

**Police fire on mobs in 1919**

**AFGHANISTAN**

**KASHMIR**

Peshawar
Gujranwala

Amritsar

**1922-1924 Reign of terror under Sikh Akhali sect**

**T I B E T**

**P U N J A B**

**N E P A L**

**1922 Civil disobedience volunteers murder 21 policemen**

**14 April 1920 Bombs dropped on Indian rioters**

**23 April 1930 Indian troops refuse British orders to fire on Indians**

**UNITED PROVINCES**

**1919 British troops kill 379 unarmed Indians**

**GUJARAT**

**BIHAR**

**BENGAL**

Police fire on mobs in 1919

**I N D I A**

Dandi

**April-May 1930 Gandhi leads protest march against British salt monopoly**

**HYDERABAD**

**1944 Famine. 1,500,000 deaths**

**1921 Moplah rising. Violence against both Hindus and Europeans. 3,000 Moplahs killed.**

**MYSORE**

**TRAVANCORE**

**CEYLON**

Indian violence against British rule 1919–1924

1924–1932

1937–1939

Violence and mass civil disobedience covered all India with the growth of the Quit India Movement in 1942

Hindu-Muslim riots both before and after the British left India in 1947 resulted in almost 2 million deaths

0        300
Miles

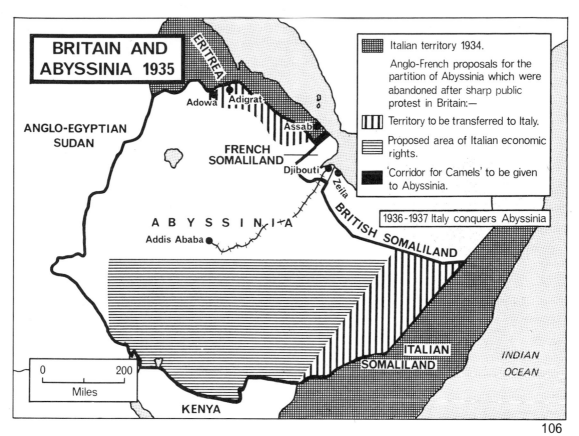

## BRITAIN AND ABYSSINIA 1935

**ANGLO-EGYPTIAN SUDAN**

ERITREA

Adowa Adigrat

Assab

FRENCH SOMALILAND

Djibouti

Zeila

A B Y S S I N I A

Addis Ababa

BRITISH SOMALILAND

ITALIAN SOMALILAND

INDIAN OCEAN

KENYA

0        200
Miles

▓ Italian territory 1934.

Anglo-French proposals for the partition of Abyssinia which were abandoned after sharp public protest in Britain:—

▥ Territory to be transferred to Italy.

▤ Proposed area of Italian economic rights.

■ 'Corridor for Camels' to be given to Abyssinia.

| 1936-1937 Italy conquers Abyssinia |

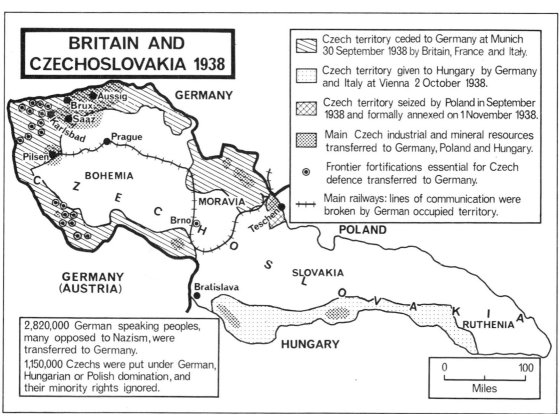

## BRITAIN AND CZECHOSLOVAKIA 1938

GERMANY

Aussig
Brüx
Saaz
Karlsbad
Prague
Pilsen
BOHEMIA
C Z E C H O S L O V A K I A
MORAVIA
Brno
Teschen
POLAND
GERMANY (AUSTRIA)
Bratislava
SLOVAKIA
HUNGARY
RUTHENIA

▨ Czech territory ceded to Germany at Munich 30 September 1938 by Britain, France and Italy.

▢ Czech territory given to Hungary by Germany and Italy at Vienna 2 October 1938.

▩ Czech territory seized by Poland in September 1938 and formally annexed on 1 November 1938.

▦ Main Czech industrial and mineral resources transferred to Germany, Poland and Hungary.

◉ Frontier fortifications essential for Czech defence transferred to Germany.

╫ Main railways: lines of communication were broken by German occupied territory.

2,820,000 German speaking peoples, many opposed to Nazism, were transferred to Germany.

1,150,000 Czechs were put under German, Hungarian or Polish domination, and their minority rights ignored.

0        100
Miles

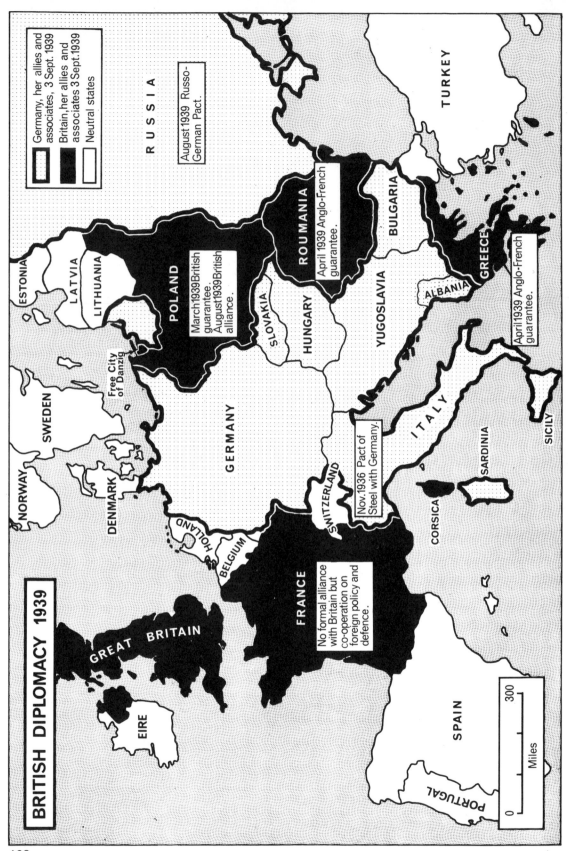

# BRITISH DIPLOMACY 1939

**Legend:**
- Germany, her allies and associates, 3 Sept. 1939
- Britain, her allies and associates 3 Sept.1939
- Neutral states

August 1939 Russo-German Pact.

POLAND — March1939British guarantee. August1939British alliance.

ROUMANIA — April 1939 Anglo-French guarantee.

GREECE — April1939 Anglo-French guarantee.

ITALY — Nov.1936 Pact of Steel with Germany.

FRANCE — No formal alliance with Britain but co-operation on foreign policy and defence.

RUSSIA

TURKEY

BULGARIA

ALBANIA

YUGOSLAVIA

HUNGARY

SLOVAKIA

ESTONIA

LATVIA

LITHUANIA

Free City of Danzig

SWEDEN

GERMANY

NORWAY

DENMARK

HOLLAND

BELGIUM

SWITZERLAND

CORSICA

SARDINIA

SICILY

GREAT BRITAIN

EIRE

SPAIN

PORTUGAL

Miles

0    300

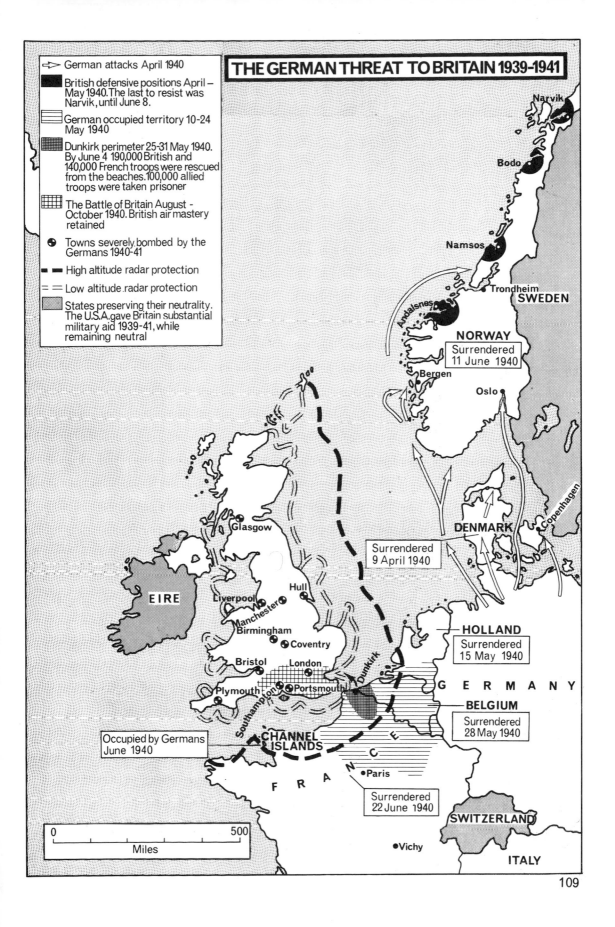

# THE GERMAN THREAT TO BRITAIN 1939-1941

**Legend:**

- ⇨ German attacks April 1940
- British defensive positions April – May 1940. The last to resist was Narvik, until June 8.
- German occupied territory 10-24 May 1940
- Dunkirk perimeter 25-31 May 1940. By June 4 190,000 British and 140,000 French troops were rescued from the beaches. 100,000 allied troops were taken prisoner
- The Battle of Britain August - October 1940. British air mastery retained
- ⊕ Towns severely bombed by the Germans 1940-41
- High altitude radar protection
- Low altitude radar protection
- States preserving their neutrality. The U.S.A. gave Britain substantial military aid 1939-41, while remaining neutral

Narvik

Bodo

Namsos

Andalsnes

Trondheim

**SWEDEN**

**NORWAY**
Surrendered 11 June 1940

Bergen

Oslo

Copenhagen

Glasgow

**EIRE**

Hull

Liverpool

Manchester

Birmingham

⊕ Coventry

Bristol

London

Plymouth

Southampton

Portsmouth

Dunkirk

**DENMARK**
Surrendered 9 April 1940

**HOLLAND**
Surrendered 15 May 1940

**G E R M A N Y**

**BELGIUM**
Surrendered 28 May 1940

Occupied by Germans June 1940

**CHANNEL ISLANDS**

**F R A N C E**

Paris

Surrendered 22 June 1940

**SWITZERLAND**

•Vichy

**ITALY**

0 _____ 500
Miles

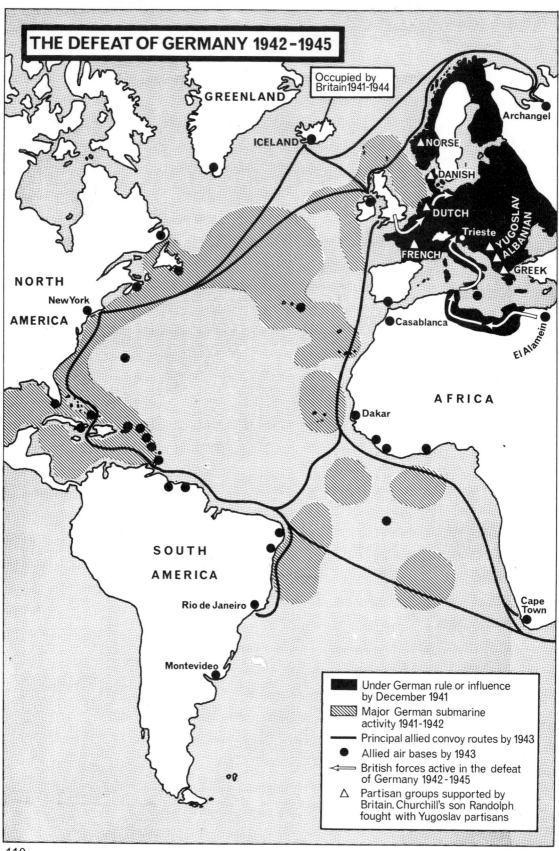

# THE DEFEAT OF GERMANY 1942-1945

GREENLAND

Occupied by
Britain 1941-1944

ICELAND

Archangel

▲ NORSE

▲ DANISH

NORTH

DUTCH

YUGOSLAV
ALBANIAN

New York

Trieste

AMERICA

FRENCH

GREEK

Casablanca

AFRICA

El Alamein

Dakar

SOUTH

AMERICA

Rio de Janeiro

Cape
Town

Montevideo

Under German rule or influence
by December 1941

Major German submarine
activity 1941-1942

Principal allied convoy routes by 1943

● Allied air bases by 1943

⇐ British forces active in the defeat
of Germany 1942-1945

△ Partisan groups supported by
Britain. Churchill's son Randolph
fought with Yugoslav partisans

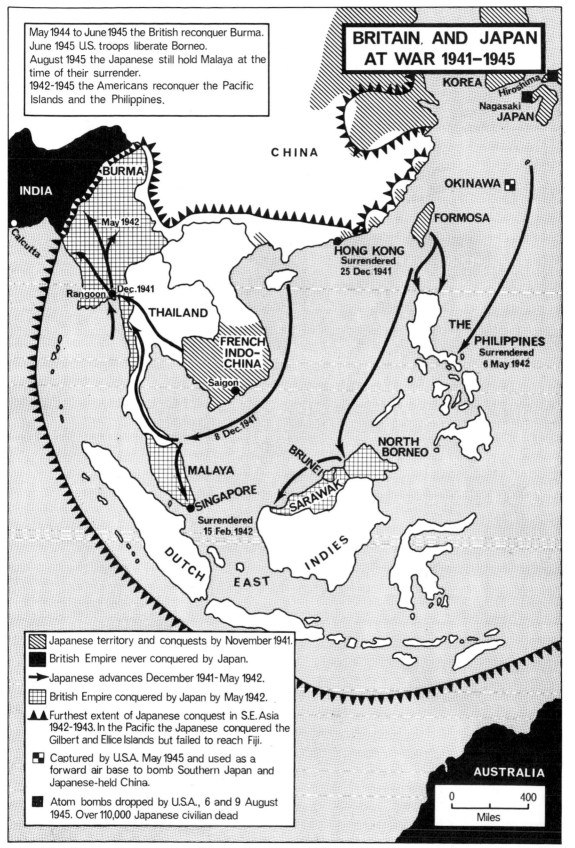

May 1944 to June 1945 the British reconquer Burma.
June 1945 U.S. troops liberate Borneo.
August 1945 the Japanese still hold Malaya at the time of their surrender.
1942-1945 the Americans reconquer the Pacific Islands and the Philippines.

# BRITAIN, AND JAPAN AT WAR 1941–1945

KOREA

Hiroshima

Nagasaki
JAPAN

CHINA

OKINAWA

BURMA

FORMOSA

INDIA

Calcutta

May 1942

HONG KONG
Surrendered
25 Dec 1941

Rangoon  Dec. 1941

THAILAND

FRENCH
INDO-
CHINA

Saigon

THE
PHILIPPINES
Surrendered
6 May 1942

8 Dec 1941

MALAYA

BRUNEI

NORTH
BORNEO

SINGAPORE
Surrendered
15 Feb. 1942

SARAWAK

DUTCH   EAST   INDIES

AUSTRALIA

Japanese territory and conquests by November 1941.

British Empire never conquered by Japan.

Japanese advances December 1941-May 1942.

British Empire conquered by Japan by May 1942.

Furthest extent of Japanese conquest in S.E. Asia 1942-1943. In the Pacific the Japanese conquered the Gilbert and Ellice Islands but failed to reach Fiji.

Captured by U.S.A. May 1945 and used as a forward air base to bomb Southern Japan and Japanese-held China.

Atom bombs dropped by U.S.A., 6 and 9 August 1945. Over 110,000 Japanese civilian dead

0        400
Miles

111

British occupation zones in Germany and Austria 1945–48.

European Free Trade Association (EFTA) 1958.

Associate Members of EFTA.

The "Iron Curtain".

European Common Market established by the Treaty of Rome 1957. Britain's first application in 1962 rejected. Second application made in 1967.

Members of the North Atlantic Treaty Organisation (NATO) established 1949. The USA and Canada are also members. Turkey was admitted 1951.

0        400
Miles

FINLAND
February 1947
Anglo–Soviet Peace Treaty limits Army to 34,000 men and Air Force to 60 machines

SWEDEN

NORWAY

U. S. S. R.

DENMARK

EIRE

NETHERLANDS

Berlin

POLAND

GREAT BRITAIN

GERMAN DEMOCRATIC REPUBLIC

GERMAN

FEDERAL

CZECHOSLOVAKIA

BELGIUM

LUXEMBOURG

REPUBLIC

HUNGARY

RUMANIA

FRANCE

AUSTRIA

SWITZ.

YUGOSLAVIA

BULGARIA

ITALY

ALBANIA

SPAIN

PORTUGAL

GREECE

GIBRALTAR
Anglo–Spanish dispute over sovereignty

**BRITAIN AND EUROPE 1945–1965**

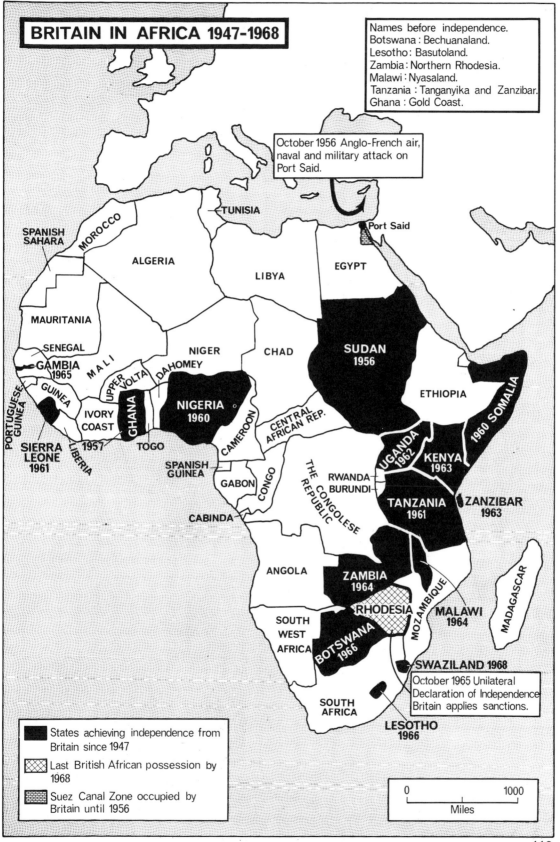

# BRITAIN IN AFRICA 1947–1968

Names before independence.
Botswana : Bechuanaland.
Lesotho: Basutoland.
Zambia : Northern Rhodesia.
Malawi : Nyasaland.
Tanzania : Tanganyika and Zanzibar.
Ghana : Gold Coast.

October 1956 Anglo-French air, naval and military attack on Port Said.

SPANISH SAHARA

MOROCCO

TUNISIA

Port Said

ALGERIA

LIBYA

EGYPT

MAURITANIA

SENEGAL

GAMBIA 1965

MALI

NIGER

CHAD

SUDAN 1956

ETHIOPIA

GUINEA

UPPER VOLTA

DAHOMEY

1960 SOMALIA

PORTUGUESE GUINEA

IVORY COAST

GHANA

NIGERIA 1960

SIERRA LEONE 1961

LIBERIA

1957

TOGO

CAMEROON

CENTRAL AFRICAN REP.

UGANDA 1962

KENYA 1963

SPANISH GUINEA

GABON

CONGO

THE CONGOLESE REPUBLIC

RWANDA
BURUNDI

CABINDA

TANZANIA 1961

ZANZIBAR 1963

ANGOLA

ZAMBIA 1964

MADAGASCAR

SOUTH WEST AFRICA

RHODESIA

MOZAMBIQUE

MALAWI 1964

BOTSWANA 1966

SWAZILAND 1968

October 1965 Unilateral Declaration of Independence Britain applies sanctions.

SOUTH AFRICA

LESOTHO 1966

States achieving independence from Britain since 1947

Last British African possession by 1968

Suez Canal Zone occupied by Britain until 1956

0        1000
Miles

113

# UNIVERSITY FOUNDATIONS 1264–1967

0    50
Miles

Aberdeen 1495

Dundee 1967

St. Andrews 1410

1967 Stirling

Glasgow 1451

Strathclyde 1964

Edinburgh 1583

Heriot-Watt 1966

Newcastle 1963

Durham 1832

Lancaster 1964

York 1963

Leeds 1904

Hull 1954

Bradford 1966

Liverpool 1903

Manchester 1851

Sheffield 1905

Salford 1967

Bangor

Keele 1962

Nottingham 1938

1966 Loughborough

Leicester 1957

East Anglia 1964

Aston 1966

Birmingham 1900

University of Wales 1893

Warwick 1965

Cambridge 1284

Aberystwyth

Essex 1965

Oxford 1264

Brunel 1966

Reading 1926

Swansea

Surrey 1966

London 1836

Cardiff

The City University 1966

Kent 1965

Bristol 1909

Bath 1966

Southampton 1952

Sussex 1961

Exeter 1955

● Founded 1264–1583
◉ Nineteenth century foundations
◉ Founded 1900–1938
◉ Founded 1952–1967

114

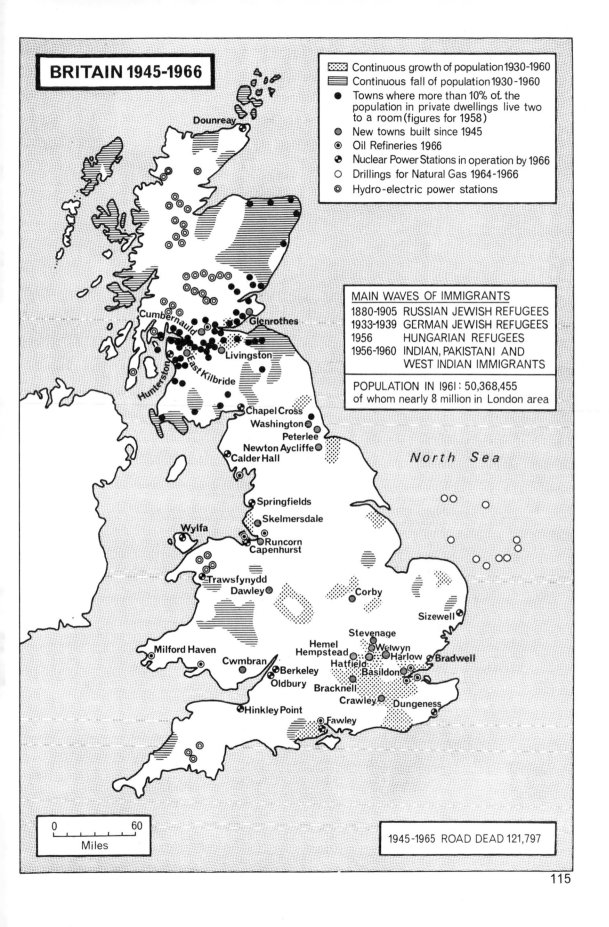

# BRITAIN 1945-1966

Continuous growth of population 1930-1960
Continuous fall of population 1930-1960
● Towns where more than 10% of the population in private dwellings live two to a room (figures for 1958)
◉ New towns built since 1945
◉ Oil Refineries 1966
◉ Nuclear Power Stations in operation by 1966
○ Drillings for Natural Gas 1964-1966
◉ Hydro-electric power stations

### MAIN WAVES OF IMMIGRANTS

1880-1905 RUSSIAN JEWISH REFUGEES
1933-1939 GERMAN JEWISH REFUGEES
1956       HUNGARIAN REFUGEES
1956-1960 INDIAN, PAKISTANI AND
            WEST INDIAN IMMIGRANTS

POPULATION IN 1961: 50,368,455
of whom nearly 8 million in London area

Dounreay

Cumbernauld
Glenrothes
East Kilbride
Livingston
Hunterston

North Sea

Chapel Cross
Washington
Peterlee
Newton Aycliffe
Calder Hall

Springfields

Skelmersdale

Wylfa
Runcorn
Capenhurst

Trawsfynydd
Dawley
Corby

Sizewell

Stevenage
Hemel
Hempstead
Welwyn
Harlow
Bradwell
Hatfield
Basildon
Bracknell
Crawley
Dungeness

Milford Haven
Cwmbran
Berkeley
Oldbury

Hinkley Point
Fawley

0 ____ 60
Miles

1945-1965 ROAD DEAD 121,797

115

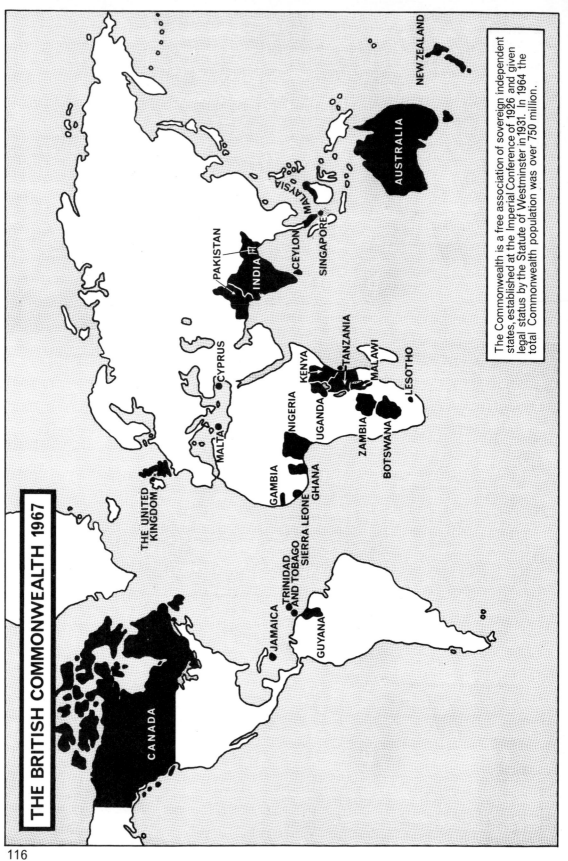

THE BRITISH COMMONWEALTH 1967

The Commonwealth is a free association of sovereign independent states, established at the Imperial Conference of 1926 and given legal status by the Statute of Westminster in 1931. In 1964 the total Commonwealth population was over 750 million.

CANADA

THE UNITED KINGDOM

JAMAICA
TRINIDAD AND TOBAGO
SIERRA LEONE
GUYANA

MALTA
CYPRUS
GAMBIA
NIGERIA
GHANA
UGANDA

PAKISTAN
INDIA
CEYLON
SINGAPORE
MALAYSIA

KENYA
TANZANIA
MALAWI
ZAMBIA
BOTSWANA
LESOTHO

AUSTRALIA

NEW ZEALAND

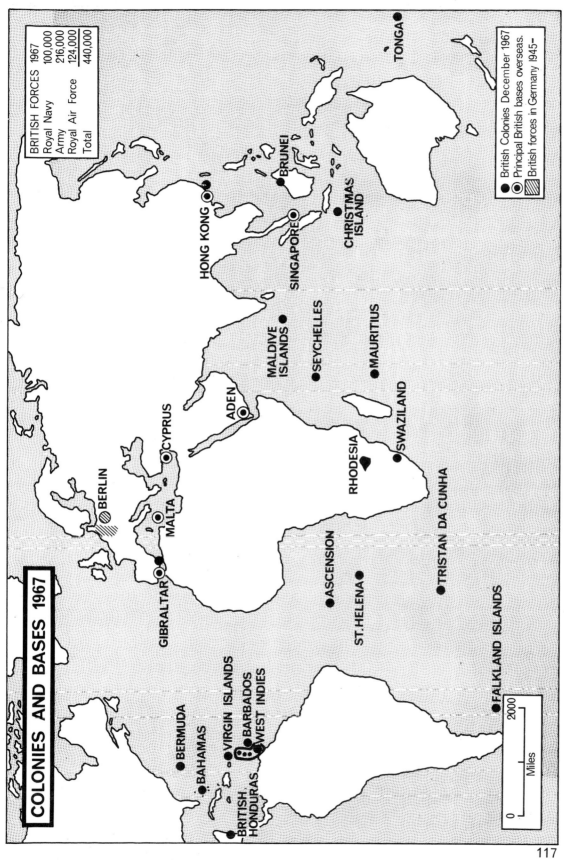

# COLONIES AND BASES 1967

BRITISH FORCES 1967
| | |
|---|---|
| Royal Navy | 100,000 |
| Army | 216,000 |
| Royal Air Force | 124,000 |
| Total | 440,000 |

● British Colonies December 1967
◉ Principal British bases overseas.
▨ British forces in Germany 1945–

BERLIN

GIBRALTAR
MALTA
CYPRUS
ADEN

HONG KONG
BRUNEI
SINGAPORE
CHRISTMAS ISLAND
TONGA

MALDIVE ISLANDS
SEYCHELLES
MAURITIUS
SWAZILAND
RHODESIA

ASCENSION
ST. HELENA
TRISTAN DA CUNHA

BERMUDA
BAHAMAS
VIRGIN ISLANDS
BARBADOS
WEST INDIES
BRITISH HONDURAS

FALKLAND ISLANDS

Miles
0                    2000

# THE WESTERN PACIFIC SINCE 1945

ALASKA
*49th U.S. STATE*

ALEUTIAN ISLANDS

U.S.S.R.

*50th U.S. STATE*

HAWAIIAN ISLANDS

MIDWAY

JOHNSTON

JAPAN

CHINA

*U.S. MILITARY ADMINISTRATION*

Hong Kong

OKINAWA  DAITO  BONIN  VOLCANO  MARCUS

WAKE

FORMOSA

VIET-NAM

PHILLIPINES

MARIANAS ISLANDS
GUAM

BIKINI

*U.S. TRUST TERRITORY*

Brunei

YAP
PALAU

ISLANDS

ENIWETOK
TRUK
MARSHALL ISLANDS

CAROLINE

BORNEO

INDONESIA

NEW GUINEA

TO AUSTRALIA

GILBERT ISLANDS

HOWLAND
BAKER

1892   CANTON ISLAND

OCEAN ISLAND
1900

ELLICE ISLANDS

1939

PHOENIX ISLANDS
1937

SOLOMON ISLANDS 1893

SANTA CRUZ ISLANDS 1898

NEW HEBRIDES
FRENCH

1887

FRENCH

AUSTRALIA

FIJI 1874

SAMOA
TUTUILA

TO NEW ZEALAND

NEW CALEDONIA

TONGA 1900

KERMADEC
TO NEW ZEALAND

COOK

NEW ZEALAND

TO NEW ZEALAND
CHATHAM

British possessions with date of acquisition.

Anglo-French Condominium.

Anglo-American joint sovereignty.

United States possessions.

Commonwealth possessions.

0        500
Miles approx.